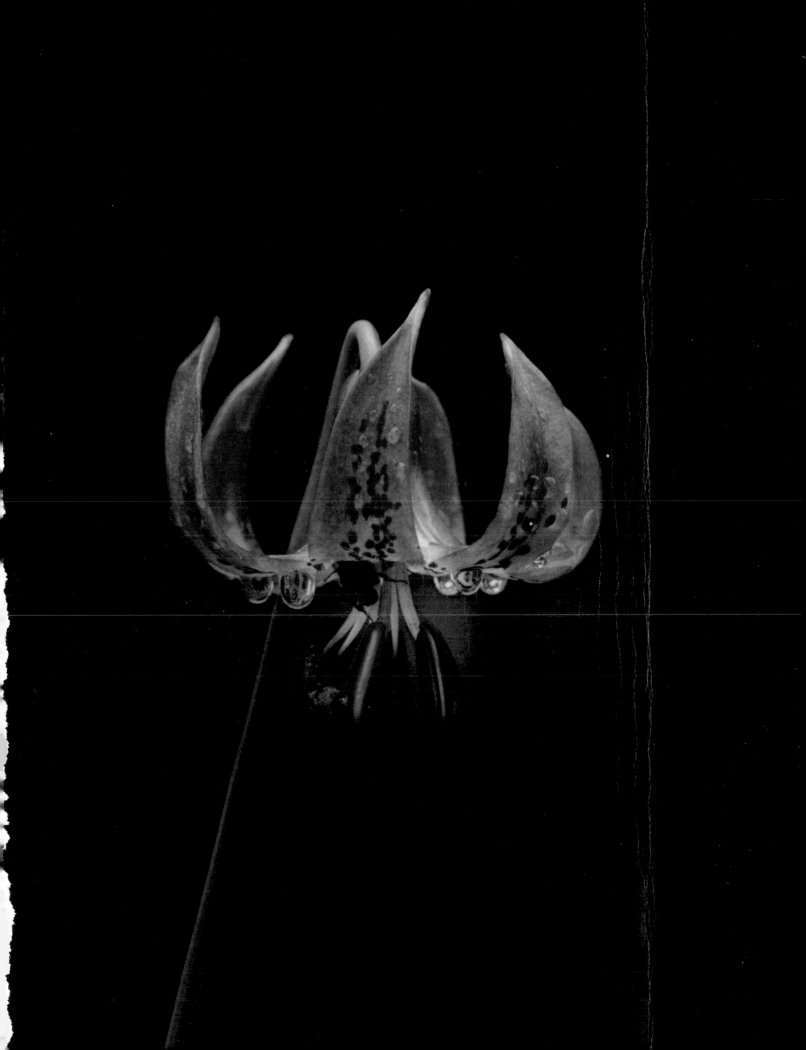

MICHIGAN NATURE ASSOCIATION

IN RETROSPECT

Celebrating 28 years of preserving Michigan's wild
and rare natural lands
1960-1988

Edited by
Bertha A. Daubendiek and Edna S. Newnan

Dwarf Lake Iris
(Iris lacustris)

Copyright © 1988 by Michigan Nature Association
All rights reserved.

Library of Congress Catalog Card Number 88-62060

Editors: Bertha A. Daubendiek and Edna S. Newnan

Editorial Committee: Dolly Katz, Kernie L. King, Lyle A. Rizor, Forbes Sibley,
        and Bette Jane Wogen

Layout and Design: Edna S. Newnan

Maps: Alan Bliss

Text by: the editors and committee members, with Tottie Catoni, Gary
        Giannunzio, Richard W. Holzman, Alice Honea, Florence Lewis,
        Ralph O'Reilly, Robert Pleznac, Mason C. Schafer, John Sohlden, and
        Adrienne Yale-Watts

The editors gratefully acknowledge proofing assistance from:
        Susan R. Crispin, Michigan Natural Features Inventory
        Dr. Anton A. Reznicek, University of Michigan Herbarium
        Dr. Ken Ross, Adrian College

Supplemental funding for publication of this book was provided by Ardis
Moore, the McColl-Batts Foundation, and the estates of Frances Broehl
and Mary Tapley.

The Michigan Nature Association salutes those hundreds who helped along the
way and have no mention in this book, especially:
        members of the press
        donors of land and funds
        MNA members and volunteers

Jacket photos: front—Forbes Sibley, *"View from Bare Bluff,"* MNA Grinnell
        Memorial Nature Sanctuary, Keweenaw

        back—Kernie L. King, *"Green Frog on Lily Pad"*

Front endpaper: Kernie L. King, *"Michigan Lily"*

The frontispiece: Kernie L. King, *"A Driftwood Happening,"* on the shore of the
        MNA Lake Superior Nature Sanctuary

Graphic Design: Roseann Dawson & Associates, Detroit

Printed by: Wintor-Swan Associates, Inc., 1614 Clay Avenue, Detroit, MI 48211

The publication of this book was supported
by funds given in memory of:

Bertha Krejci and
Carl H. Daubendiek
(parents of Bertha A. Daubendiek)

Jay Gordon Hall

Walter P. Nickell

Isabel and Myron Zucker

"Here, I need something to show size. Can you just put your finger down?" John Sohlden asked his companion Bertha Daubendiek while taking pictures at Grass Lake Nature Sanctuary, May 23, 1987. This picture is symbolic in two ways: Bertha has had her finger in every project of the Michigan Nature Association since its beginning in 1952. (Her short-clipped nails show readiness to tackle problems in no-nonsense fashion!) And, the dwarf lake iris has been the official logo since 1970 of the MNA, a non-profit organization dedicated to the preservation of Michigan's native flora and fauna.

Preface

On June 28, 1987, fifty happy people gathered in the coolness of a stately hemlock grove near the shore of Lake Superior to dedicate the 100th project of the Michigan Nature Association—the Twin Waterfalls Nature Preserve in Munising. It was a precious moment in the organization's 35-year history. The group sat quietly as founder Bertha Daubendiek read the names of 138 loved ones in whose honor contributions had been given toward the purchase of the MNA Memorial Waterfalls. Later that day, a private dedication was held for the Rudy M. Olson Memorial Waterfalls (opposite page).

The falls are in adjacent canyons with two different creeks flowing through them. They are surrounded by 15 acres of untouched northern woods punctuated by cliff outcroppings. Although close together, the canyons have different aspects. The Olson site is choked with vegetation including small mountain maples, silvery spleenwort fern, and plants that grow only in undisturbed soil—giant twisted-stalk, and native orchids such as striped coral-root. The other canyon is more open. A delightful park-like path at its top leads through a handsome grove of American beech trees. Beech-drops, a plant parasitic on beech roots, are plentiful here.

The establishment of the Association's 100th sanctuary is an appropriate time to look back on the group's achievements. This book, then, celebrates how a handful of nature advocates, armed with little more than dedication and vision, have achieved the near-impossible in preserving their state's natural heritage. It shows the accomplishments of the hard-working members of the organization who, through generous donations of time and money—and not a single penny of government funds—have devoted the past 28 years to searching out and protecting exemplary remnants of Michigan's original wild lands. Such a systematic effort is unequaled elsewhere.

The book also spotlights 26 of the MNA's most popular, accessible, and easiest-to-find properties, as well as describing some of the more challenging ones. It shows the pride that members and supporters feel for Michigan—its forests and prairies, its lakes, dunes and rock formations, and, above all, its amazing variety of plants and animals.

Natural areas, once severely modified, can never be recreated. We hope the MNA story will inspire people in other states to start similar preservation programs.

1 & 2. *Presiding at the dedication of the Twin Falls Nature Preserve were Bertha Daubendiek, executive secretary of the MNA, and Richard W. Holzman, ten-year past president, current president, and speaker of the day.*

3. *The MNA Twin Waterfalls Preserve is a piece of the Munising sandstone formation, estimated to be 550 million years old. The canyon walls are covered with ferns and liverworts that thrive on the constant moisture produced by falling spray and water seeping through the rocks.*

4. *The slender cliff-brake fern, Cryptogramma stelleri (T), has delicate fronds 3½ to 7 inches long. A rare fern, it is abundant at Twin Falls.*

Legend

(E)—Endangered ⎱ species status under the Michigan Endangered
(T)—Threatened ⎰ Species Act as of January 1988

(SC)—Of Special Concern. While not afforded legal protection under
the Act, the species are rare in Michigan because of declining
or relict populations in the state.

(E—USA) ⎱ Endangered or Threatened with extinction in what-
(T—USA) ⎰ ever state it was ever found, protected under the
Federal Endangered Species Act as of January 1988

MNA Sanctuary classification

"A"—easiest to visit
"B"—not easy; best to go on a guided field trip here first
"C"—cannot be visited without a guide

Abbreviations

N.S.—nature sanctuary 20 acres or more
P.P.—plant preserve under 20 acres
Mem.—memorial
UP—Upper Peninsula
LP—Lower Peninsula

Contents

Ring Around Detroit

Within a radius of 35 miles from the traffic din, polluted air, and paved-over land of one of the nation's largest metropolitan areas is a dense white cedar swamp that looks much as it did when the land was inhabited only by wandering tribes of Indians. The Lakeville Swamp Nature Sanctuary (opposite) is one of many MNA preserves within easy driving distance of Detroit.

More than six million people—72 percent of Michigan's total population—live in the 22 southeastern counties shown on the map. A person raised in such a congested area may often yearn for a quiet place that retains some of the natural beauty that existed throughout Michigan before so much was altered and destroyed by human activity. The "Ring Around Detroit," an emerald necklace of MNA sanctuaries, fulfills that yearning.

The present-day face of southeastern Michigan was molded 10,000 to 15,000 years ago by deposits left as the last glacier retreated. Blocks of ice became lakes, and melt-water formed streams. Plant life gradually re-established itself. Eventually magnificent hardwood forests appeared on the fertile glacial till. White pine grew to enormous proportions on sandy ridges and plains from St. Clair County northward.

In the 1780's, when the first Europeans arrived, dense woods and impenetrable swamps covered most of the region. Wolf, bear, and lynx ranged near the settlers' dwellings; wild turkey, bald eagle, and passenger pigeons were abundant. A century later, fifty years of intense lumbering had transformed the face of southeastern Michigan from wilderness to cleared land. Farming acreage in turn was converted to residential and commercial uses as Detroit grew into an industrial giant. Today, at one of the metro-area's busiest traffic centers—Telegraph and Long Lake Roads in Oakland County—90,000 cars pass every 24 hours where Indians once tracked game.

In 1960, members of the Macomb Nature Association (forerunner of the MNA), alarmed by the continued destruction of their area's few remaining patches of natural beauty, took action. They voted to change their group's emphasis from one of nature study and education to a program of purchasing remnants of natural land outright to keep them forever undeveloped. This shift in policy was sparked when it became evident that local public park authorities were actually destroying the very species in need of protection, and that state agencies and other conservation groups were doing little to come to their defense.

The first MNA sanctuaries established were all near the Detroit metropolitan area: four in St. Clair County and one—the Lakeville Swamp—in Oakland County.

Stoney Creek flowing through wetlands at Lakeville Swamp Nature Sanctuary.

Photo by John Sohlden, biology teacher of Clintondale Schools, who writes:

"In late afternoon on a mild October day, I put on my high rubber boots and walked out into the swamp, making my way around the hummocks of Carex aquatilla. On the banks of the creek were clumps of meadow sweet and thickets of red osier dogwood. As I took the picture and dusk came on, I became more and more cautious of where to place my feet, since I had come across massasaugas in the area on earlier trips. Sure enough! Just as I was stepping down with my right foot I made out the silhouette of a coiled rattler and heard its warning buzz. It was time to pack my gear and beat a rapid retreat to the safety of high ground! As I walked back to the road I could see the masses of tamarack and quaking aspen in the distance, lit up in their autumn cloth-of-gold."

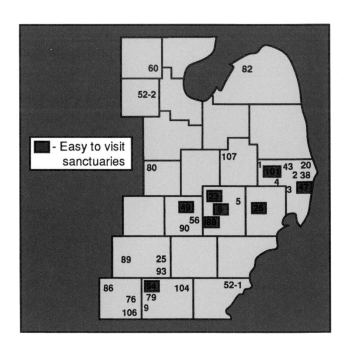

There are now 33 MNA-established nature sanctuaries and preserves in this 22-county area.

1. *A large, deceptively flat-looking expanse of the swamp, known ecologically as a "southern wet meadow," is composed of large clumps of sedge on land never plowed or disturbed by man. The individual plants are old, tall, and closely spaced. To make your way through these ancient water-logged hummocks is taxing; they are real ankle-twisters. In mid-April the hummocks can be seen from the east side of Rochester Road where it crosses through the swamp. In summer and fall the sedge meadow greens up, creating an illusion of unbroken level land (5—center).*

2. *In winter it looks like this: huge obstacles at every step.*

3. *Showy lady-slipper or Queen's lady-slipper, Cypripedium reginae, grows by the hundreds in colonies that can be seen on an annual guided tour in late June.*

4. *A half-dozen species of native orchids grow in hidden places in the swamp. One is the small white lady-slipper, Cypripedium candidum (T, T-USA).*

12

Lakeville Swamp Nature Sanctuary

This Project No. 5 exemplifies the role of the MNA program from the very first in preserving vital natural wetlands. The Swamp extends through a valley three miles from east to west. The only vehicle crossing is a 1200-foot stretch of the Rochester Road built by early settlers and still used today. To the east is southern wet meadow; to the west, white cedar swamp. The sanctuary is not presented here as an easy area to visit. On the contrary, it is designated as "class C", requiring a guide. Nonetheless, it is one of the easiest properties to find and visually enjoy from perimeter roads.

Located close to a large population, Lakeville remains the "Unconquered Swamp"—a wilderness at our very doorstep.

Just 35 miles as the crow flies from the shining towers of Detroit's Renaissance Center, it is still the morass which the French author, Alexis DeTocqueville, described in his 1837 journal. Here the intruder learns to rely on his compass, and reckon with mosquitoes, poison sumac, and rattlesnakes.

The spring-fed muck of the Swamp maintains the environment for hard-to-find plants that once were common in Michigan. Opened to the public in 1963, the Sanctuary is a refuge for hawks, water-loving birds, over 500 species of native plants, the Massasauga rattlesnake, and is also headwaters of Stoney Creek. Michigan's largest poison sumac and black haw tree grow here, as does the National Champion American or wild plum.

A SWAMP WORTH SAVING: THE ROAD DILEMMA.

Few people deliberately choose to venture into the Swamp. Indeed, there is only one place where access is fairly easy to see large stands of showy lady-slippers and a precious tiny fen on a short walk. Here, in spring, the stream-bank is aglow with marsh marigolds, and the mossy path leads through blooming wildflowers including twinflower and clintonia, unusual this far south.

It was this very spot, however, where, in 1986, the Oakland County Road Commission (OCRC) proposed to put through a new road. When MNA learned of this plan, it mobilized volunteers and other local supporters to spring into action: they counted birds, cars, trucks, plants, and trees. They suggested that traffic—up to 5,000 vehicles including hundreds of loaded gravel trucks thundering through the swamp every 24 hours—be diverted to other routes; they recommended widening the present road, putting up signs to slow traffic, and modifying corner angles.

The environmentalist hired by OCRC reported that the site of the proposed road was the most ecologically sensitive of any land owned by the commission. He found it contained both boreal and southern floral types, and concluded that the area "appears to be the largest and most species-rich remaining of this community-type in Oakland County and perhaps in southern Michigan"—an evaluation later corroborated by the 1987 Michigan Natural Features Inventory.

Meanwhile a "Society of Swamp Angels," raised money to purchase an additional ten acres located along the proposed right-of-way, a tract which had been a "hold-out" when the MNA obtained the original 66.35 acres.

After 18 months of patient field work, negotiation, and persuasion, the road dilemma was amicably settled by working out a restrained improvement of the present roadway.

Swamps are among our last natural areas. They are irreplaceable water reservoirs and hideouts for endangered wildlife. With the tackling of the Lakeville project it became clear that this type of preservation was the right path for the organization to pursue, and that public support from both members and non-members could be gained.

Lakeville Swamp has stood the test of time. By any standard, it is one of the most valuable MNA properties.

Please drive out and see it for yourself.

Wilcox-Warnes Memorial Nature Sanctuary

A botanist could study this woods every day for a year and still not exhaust the sanctuary's treasures. Located only six miles from Lakeside Mall at M-59 and Schoenherr, it is a splendid deciduous hardwood forest with American beech and tulip poplar predominant. In addition, a visitor on an afternoon stroll could identify red maple, white ash, white oak, basswood, yellow birch, black walnut, and shagbark hickory. Hawks, screech owls, and great horned owls nest here.

The woods beauty changes with the seasons. The fall color is splendid. In winter, a hiker tracking through snow may see the leaves of young beech trees looking almost poppy-colored in the rays of the low-lying sun.

Bette Jane Wogen and her late husband John, visited Harold Warnes, property donor, almost weekly for five years, and led many field trips here. "The elderly Mr. Warnes was delighted to walk the trails with us through the masses of spring flowers—white and red trillium, dwarf ginseng, foamflower, hepatica, May-apple, and many others. John was the first person to find showy orchis plants, blooming in late May. The woods is perfect for the study of birds, ferns, and mushrooms."

Fringed and bottle gentian, cardinal flower, two varieties of skullcap, and square-stemmed monkey-flower are among plants that appear later. A few specimen of the large round-leaved orchid—normally found only much farther north—also grow here. The orchid's two large basal leaves can be up to eight inches across.

Indian arrowheads and scrapers have been found in the open area to the north.

1 & 2. *The southern 27 acres of Wilcox-Warnes was never grazed, and is especially noted for its fine grove of more than 400 tulip trees in various stages. Although often called yellow poplar, this species actually belongs to the magnolia family. Massive trunks with slate-gray, deeply-furrowed bark stand straight as lodge poles. Look up into the outside crown of this tree in early June and you will see exotic tawny-colored blooms on the branches, appearing like lit sconces on some gigantic candelabra in the sky. The leaves, which emerge before the flowers, have a broad base and almost square tips notched in the middle.*

3. *Photographer Pat Cimarosti hiked into the woods very early on the clear frosty morning of October 18, 1986, to catch these red maple leaves etched with a tracery of frost.*

4. *John Sohlden comments, "To capture a 'great shot' I took up to 200 exposures on several trips to Warnes Woods. These trees grow in a vernal pond which dries up only in the heat of July and August. In spring the green moss glows against the base of the trunks; large white trillium, wake robin, hepatica, and Jack-in-the-pulpit grow at pond's edge. In the moist thickets, along the edge of the woods, I would often hear the 'peent' of the American woodcock and the occasional drumming of the ruffed grouse trying to get the attention of a would-be mate."*

Species in picture are: the small smooth-barked tree with leaves (left foreground) is a young beech, the large trunk (center) is a white oak, and next to it is a red maple.

1

2

3

Clifford R. and Calla C. Burr Memorial Plant Preserve

This preserve in Rose Township, Oakland County, is small in size—only 5.01 acres—but large in variety. A visitor can see oak woods, tamaracks, a tiny stream, a meadow with an active fen, a bog with pitcher plants, wet and dry prairies, and 289 species of native plants.

The fen is a small wetland of organic soil infiltrated by cold ground water.

The week before Memorial Day masses of small white lady-slippers appear. A large stand of colicroot blooms about July 4, and there is an outstanding display of fringed gentians after mid-September.

1 *In late spring the prairie plant, hoary puccoon, grows in great clumps.*
2 *After a chill night, the web of an argiope spider shimmers in the morning light.*
3 *A frosty morning at the preserve.*
4 *(top, left, opposite page) A dragonfly and its perch of golden Alexanders are covered with a silver filigree of dew.*

16

4

Southeast Michigan Specialties

5 The twinleaf, Jeffersonia diphylla (SC), blooms on a steep hillside at the Shiawassee River Plant Preserve. A hike of half a mile back to the bluff overlooking the river is rewarded by a chance to find it in flower. It blooms early in April, at the same time as bloodroot. The leaves of the two plants are very similar in color and texture, but those of the twinleaf are deeply lobed.

The fragile white flower lasts only a few hours at the peak of its perfection before the petals fall off. Twinleaf is found now in only a few counties in the southern Lower Peninsula. It needs rich woodland soil, and many areas which formerly had large quantities have been cut over for development, shopping centers, and highways.

The plant was named after President Jefferson by his friend and fellow botanist, William Bartram.

6 The American lotus, Nelumbo lutea (T), exists in Michigan only in scattered patches in Monroe County along streams feeding into Lake Erie. The pale yellow flowers, up to eight inches across, appear in early August. Blossoms and leaves are held on tall stems up to two feet above the water.

The MNA Lotus Preserve is at the mouth of Swan Creek near one of the few remaining bits of natural shoreline on Lake Erie. Lotus will only grow in three to five feet of water, and this patch is now recovering from the ravages of the high water of 1986 and 1987.

7 MNA's first project, Red Wing Acres Nature Sanctuary in St. Clair County, is a 40-acre corner of what was once the 2200-acre Capac swamp—a natural cranberry marsh that was drained by the state in 1866.

This first venture of MNA was not strictly a natural area; although it was the last undrained part of the swamp, it had once been farmed. Safe, however, in a low wet section along a fence, slough grass, Beckmannia syzigachne (T), still grows. This patrician grass is known at only one other location in the state.

5

6

7

1

1 *At the height of the fall color season, October 18, 1986, leaves of the red maple and wild black cherry (yellow) create a palette of primary colors against an electric blue sky.*

2 *On May 5, 1979, photographer Lyle Rizor and wife Mary were walking along the floodplain when they saw a red fox kit lying in the sun, midway up a steep bank. Lyle, moving gradually closer, took several pictures with a telephoto lens before the kit became alarmed and retreated into its den.*

Shannon Nature Sanctuary

Easy-to-visit Shannon, near Parshallville in Livingston County, is a comparatively small area containing a variety of plant communities. The following listing is in order of occurrence, beginning at the entrance: a spring-fed pond, a dry, mature oak woods, a cattail marsh, a sedgy open wet corridor, a moist floodplain along a small creek, an old field regenerating to a mixed species woods, and a mature evergreen plantation.

Spring tops the seasons because of the abundance of wildflowers, song birds, and waterfowl. Large white trilliums dominate the floral display, but other familiar plants are also present. Unusual species found here are the poke milkweed, *Asclepias exaltata,* the only variety of milkweed that grows in the woods, feverwort or tinker's-weed, and a mutant variation of the white trillium which has a sterile multi-petaled blossom.

In addition to flowering plants, a vegetation list for the sanctuary includes 44 species of deciduous trees and shrubs, nine evergreens, 10 vines, and 11 ferns. Some 25 kinds of birds have been observed in their nesting habitats.

3 A view of winter in the oak woods looking back toward the entrance; it is a time of tranquility throughout the sanctuary. Here white oaks predominate, mixed with red oak, wild black cherry, and a sprinkling of aspen and witch hazel.

Irene and Elmer P. Jasper Woods Memorial Nature Sanctuary

This sanctuary is noted as one of the most quiet, restful places to be found off any paved road in Michigan. Only a little over an hour's drive from Detroit via I-94, it is a favorite of many and fun for children. A springtime visit will bring the extra bonus of a chance to view the prized painted trillium.

The mixed woods (1) can be seen as you drive or walk along an easy sand trail. In autumn, sugar and red maple leaves form a blazing backdrop for the trunks of many tree species: white oak, hemlock, white birch, sassafras, American beech, red oak, and ash.

Notice that a slight dip in elevation brings you to the moist, rich soil conditions of a northern forest, and the tree mixture changes to a classic combination of **yellow birch**, **hemlock**, and **hard maple**. As the trail drops down even further, you enter predominantly hemlock groves. We suggest that you take a compass if you decide to explore the 40 acres on the west side of the road, as there are no marked trails. (4) shows the furled golden bark of the yellow birch, at left, looking like ancient bronze artwork against feathery green hemlock branches and shiny maple leaves.

Some birds nesting at Jasper are the warbling vireo, blackburnian, mourning, and black-throated green warblers, least flycatcher, scarlet tanager, ruby-throated hummingbird, rose-breasted grosbeak, wood and mallard ducks, and several owl species.

In the low-lying wetter parts of the sanctuary grow wild ginger, foamflower, wintergreen, goldthread, dwarf ginseng, toothwort, and northern beadlily. Some ferns are royal, interrupted, cinnamon, New York, Christmas, maidenhair, and ostrich. Late summer brings Michigan holly, Indian pipe, pinesap, and cardinal flower.

A "Trillium Trilogy" takes place each springtime. The purple trillium, Trillium erectum (3), blooms first in early May, in a wet section where it is very abundant. Next appears the large-flowered trillium, T. grandiflorum. For the grand finale—in an area different from the other two— the chief botanical wonder of the sanctuary, the painted trillium, T. undulatum (E) (2), comes up amidst ground pines and wintergreen under the sweeping hemlock branches. St. Clair County is a photographers' mecca for this species, because the next closest station is in Vermont.

James and Alice Brennan Memorial Nature Sanctuary

The wide range of nature encounters that can be experienced here makes this sanctuary intriguing the year around. On a trip, Adrienne Yale-Watts commented, "What awes me is its sense of seclusion." Cut off from all cross-traffic by adjoining buffer farmlands, the visitor feels he has left the world behind.

It is possible to take just an hour's brisk romp along the two-mile marked trail, or spend an entire day in quiet observation. First comes Inspiration Grove, with its refreshing smell of pine needles. After a trek through a large clearing, you enter the floodplain of the Pine River and set out on Tinker's-weed Trail, named for the unusual plant that edges the path (5). After crossing Pine River, the trail leads for an eighth mile through heavy woods on a high bank overlooking the river, where, in the spring, there are dense mats of wildflowers.

You then traverse a bottomlands floodplain and cross the river again to a cattail marsh with hundreds of beaver workings. In mid-summer, the Pine is so crystal clear that clam trails can be seen in the sand of the boulder-strewn river bottom, and the wetlands are bright with wild iris, Michigan lilies, jewelweed and Joe-Pye-weed. Next the trail follows a loop of the river encircling a five-acre swamp.

Here in May, 1987, a hiker watched while a family of wood ducks got their first view of the world. The ducklings had pecked through their shells and stood uncertainly at the mouth of their nest cavity high up in a dead elm tree. Urged on by their mother's calls from below, the day-old fuzz-balls spread their stubby wings and plummeted to the ground, then followed her to the water for their first meal of duckweed. A month later, when the sanctuary was dedicated, leader Evelyn Dent (3), center, guided a group through the same area.

1

1 *Along the trail you might meet an enterprising garter snake—at home in almost any habitat—which hunts by day in wet vegetation for worms and small amphibians.*

2 *A serene scene along Pine River in mid-September. A yellow birch and sugar maples edge the stream on the left. Across the river on slightly higher ground is a rich, mature* **beech-maple** *woods, one of the classic habitats of Michigan. Other trees are blue beech, hickory, and basswood.*

4 *The nannyberry,* Viburnum lentago, *grows as a shrub or small tree in the damp woods and along river banks. The small white flowers, which appear in clusters in late spring, develop into dark blue fruits after going through a delicious-looking lavender stage.*

5 *The tinker's-weed has fruits like cherry tomatoes and is easily recognized by its wing-like leaves wrapped around the stem. It grows two to four feet tall.*

2

3

4 5

21

1

Timberland Swamp Nature Sanctuary

A stunning spring wildflower spectacle, a vast cathedral-like forest, and a remarkable number of bird species are major attractions at this largest showplace MNA sanctuary in southeastern Michigan, where the welcome sign (2) is always out.

This 245-acre swamp forest in Springfield Township, Oakland County, is one of the Association's earliest and most dramatic achievements. It was acquired in 11 separate purchases between 1967 and 1978. The success of this project convinced MNA members that support could be generated for large, expensive projects.

The sanctuary is part of an 800-acre backwoods wilderness that lies in a shallow, two-mile-wide basin formed 13,000 years ago by debris from the last retreating glacier. The basin, tilted from north to south, is the high water point of Oakland County. Here, many springs and small streams join to form the Huron River, which emerges as a cool trout stream at the southern edge of the swamp. The Shiawassee River and a branch of the Clinton also begin in Timberland.

Masses of wildflowers spring from the humus-rich earth in April and May. First to push through the brown cover of last year's leaves is the hepatica (3). Its delicately tinted blossoms contrast sharply with the maroon, leathery, liver-shaped leaves for which the plant is named. Later in the month, thousands of spring beauty blossoms cover the ground like a dusting of snow (1). May brings a myriad of large white trilliums.

During the growing season, the inner depths of the preserve are bathed in a diffuse green light. Avenues of giant ash, maple, and oak lead off as far as you can see in all directions. The silence is punctuated only by the husky song of a scarlet tanager, the wiry buzz of cerulean warblers, the sigh of an unfelt breeze high in the forest canopy, and the tapping of woodpeckers. Of the latter, the pileated—America's largest variety—thrives in the large expanses of climax forest; red-

3

2

WELCOME
Please help preserve this forest in unspoiled condition — for your descendants
You are our guest.
Take nothing but inspiration
Leave nothing but your cares.
DO NOT CUT PICK OR DIG
NO VEHICLES PLEASE
Michigan Nature Association

4   5

bellied, hairy, and downy woodpeckers also live here year round, as do barred, screech, and great horned owls. The brushy thickets that encircle the forest provide ideal habitats for many varieties of warblers including the blue-winged, golden-winged, Brewster's, chestnut-sided, yellow, mourning, and Canada.

Timberland is one of the few remaining tracts in southern Michigan large enough to furnish territory for the Cooper's hawk (SC) and the red-shouldered hawk (T).

The wooded areas of the preserve are an intermingling of two forest types. In the wet lowlands is a swamp forest of elm, red and silver maple, black and white ash, basswood, and yellow birch. On patches of higher ground are islands of American beech, hard maple, oak, and tulip trees, with a marvelous understory of flowers, ferns, and shrubs. One such shrub is the leatherwood, or "wicopy," which bears clusters of attractive yellow flowers in early spring. Leatherwood's bark, while soft and pliant, is so tough that it is impossible to break off a branch without tools.

The best times to visit Timberland are from April 25 to May 20, when the wildflowers peak, and from Labor Day until deep snow. Summer features great colonies of ferns growing in shoulder-high masses, but also produces obnoxious swarms of mosquitoes and beds of stinging nettles. In late summer, prairie plants like lupine, stiff goldenrod, and big bluestem grass grow along the railroad at the sanctuary's north edge. Timberland's thrilling fall color show takes place between October 1 and October 25. After the leaves have fallen, hiking continues to be rewarding, as the lay of the land is clearly visible.

Goldenseal, *Hydrastis canadensis* (T) (4), a member of the buttercup family, bears a single flower in late April. (5) shows the late Robert Kilgore, for many years MNA's chief botanist, examining a bed of goldenseal with its bright red berries in August. The Indians used the plant for medicine.

The raccoon (6) which likes a varied diet, finds plentiful hunting at Timberland: frogs and crayfish—which it often rinses in the stream before eating—fruits, nuts, insects, and bird and turtle eggs. Hollow trees or fallen logs make ideal dens. An average of four young born in early spring are big enough to fend for themselves by winter.

The peach-leaf willow, *Salix amygdaloides*, widespread but difficult to identify, grows in southern Michigan swamps and floodplains. Its fruits are smooth, its leaves long and slender, with ½ to ¾ inch long petioles. Positive identification depends on finding branchlets when the flowers have just developed into fruit.

For years, MNA people had searched in vain for just one peach-leaf willow. Then on May 5, 1985, Harvey Ballard, Jr. found a half-dozen huge old trees along the stream at the entrance bridge to Timberland. Some branchlets had fallen to earth with the fruits still attached, cinching the discovery (see closeup [7] made by Pat Cimarosti that day). Peach-leaf willows have been in Timberland all along!

6   7

Goose Creek Grasslands Nature Sanctuary

It might be supposed that nothing new could be discovered about the vegetation of Michigan, yet in the fall of 1985 a hitherto unknown large acreage of undisturbed wet grassland was found in the historic Irish Hills region of Lenawee County. Its popularity rose almost overnight to make it one of MNA's favorite "fun places."

Stretched out over a mile east and west, a wonderful diversity exists here—saturated soil, wet prairie, marsh, and fen (low land partially covered with water). The preserve is in a valley where great heaps of raw gravel have been deposited in a glacial trough with fen in the bottom, where Goose Creek gurgles clear, winding through the **wet meadow** (4) with its few trees and shrubs.

It is a safe, pleasant place to be. A person walking into the prairie can be seen at all times from the road, yet feels himself in a dream world of close intimacy with soil and sky.

Birding at Goose Creek is exquisitely satisfying. Bird song carries far across the flat prairie—mallards quacking, the "witchity" of yellowthroat, and "fitz bews" of the willow flycatcher mingle with a chorus of red wings, bobolinks, meadowlarks, and bob-whites sounding off as swallows dart overhead.

The Day We Found a Thousand Pitcher Plants—by B.A.D.

"A few times in each life there is one day that stands forever in memory. Such was the case June 6, 1986. It was a rare combination of clear skies, comfortable temperature, no bugs, and the companionship of an enthusiastic photographer. The young people who live on the edge of this special place also came along and let out squeals of delight at every new thing found. We had a goal of exploring the wettest part in the center of the sanctuary where no one ever goes. There John Sohlden was so enthralled by the sight of his first pitcher plant that he lay down to get into shooting position underneath the blossoms. I ranged far and ahead of him, sending back the youngsters with messages that hundreds and hundreds of pitcher plants lay before us. He would not budge, however, but stayed with his first clump to produce photo (2).

"Meanwhile my helpers and I were inspecting every edible valerian plant we came across. Valeriana edulis (T), was conspicuous, 3 to 4 feet tall, and there was a lot of it. However, it was also elusive in that I had stalked the plant for several weeks trying to find one in full bloom. Unfortunately either the individual blooms had already closed or were not yet fully open (like the twinleaf, V. edulis appears to stay open for only a few hours). We looked over dozens and dozens and dozens of plants. At last we made the find of a lifetime—one plant in perfect flower. We marked it and it stayed in shape until John caught up and got photo (1). The arduous trek through sedge hump and mire had been successful!"

1

2

3 *"This* Liatris spicata *(spike or dense blazing-star) and common sulphur butterfly were photographed at Goose Creek on August 17, 1986, not far from the Cement City Highway bridge. I found it while checking on the progress of prairie dropseed grass there."*
—*Mason Schafer*

4

5 *Step across the footbridge over the ditch at the side of the paved Cement City Highway and you see prairie cord grass, lobelia, shrubby cinquefoil, goldenrod, and dogwood. Placing your feet carefully around sedge humps, you follow a 12-inch wide trail; everywhere there are strange and wonderful plants. You can ask a million questions and learn a dozen new species on every trip, as you enjoy the colorful array of flowers and grasses that changes weekly from April through fall.*

A big attraction is the opportunity to see the rare, interesting prairie dropseed, Sporobolus heterolepis (T). (The clumps are to the right of the lead people in the picture.) Mason Schafer recorded the plant's progress in 1987: "Growing along the trail, it makes a nice fountain of emerald green leaves. The seed head has a faint but unmistakable fragrance detected by some people but not by others." (See page 68 for photographs of bloom and seed, which are the stages at which it is most easily recognizable. Both were taken here where dropseed grows among many other plants. At BKD Memorial, however, there are separate stands of it alone.)

6 *The prairie comes into its full glory in September and October. Here the turkeyfoot or big bluestem grass tops can be seen in the background, surrounded by various kinds of goldenrods: the stiff, called Solidago rigida, Canada, and grass-leaved.*

7 *Two varieties of gorgeous blue fringed gentians grow here, blooming August, September and into October.*

25

1

1 Swamps and floodplains are among the richest of forest types. A floodplain is the area in a creek or river bottom that is covered with the soil deposited by floods. Above shows **southern floodplain forest** habitat at Bean Creek Nature Sanctuary. The photo was taken April 7, 1985, when the water at Bean Creek was four to five feet above normal level. The tree in the foreground is a red ash; others are American elm, willow, and more red ash—all trees that can survive standing in water for varying periods of time.

2 Leaves and fruit of the Ohio buckeye, common in the lowlands. Leaves are palmately compound, with five leaflets, rarely seven.

3 The first flower to blossom at Bean Creek is the harbinger-of-spring, Erigenia bulbosa, also known as "salt and pepper," a favorite photographers' subject. About March 25 it is barely four inches tall—the above shows its size in reference to a last year's leaf. The plant soon changes into a scarcely recognizable jumble of parsley-like foliage 10 inches high and full of seeds at the top.

4 The blue ash, Fraxinus quadrangulata, is found on the floodplain. It is an unusual species in Michigan because the southern tier of counties is the northern limit of its range. It can be identified by its four-sided twigs with corky ridges or "wings." Its inner bark contains a sticky substance which turns blue when exposed to light.

5 Bean Creek is in brilliant color when the leaves are changing. With the water level down, the creek can be crossed via a fallen log as this group of latter day pioneers is demonstrating.

3

4

5

Robert Powell Memorial Nature Sanctuary
(formerly Bean Creek)

The Powell sanctuary is a wonderful one of the B type, meaning it must be visited on a guided field trip for the first time to get you acquainted with the layout. It is near the Ohio border where spring comes first to Michigan. Landlocked on the back of a farm, flooding in spring makes a long walk necessary to get in to the higher ground to see the wildflowers. By April 9 hepaticas will be in bloom, and a week later the first tree to leaf out, the Ohio buckeye, will be thrusting its pointed leaflets up like unfolding umbrellas.

The "mountain," a high circle of land that is a former creek bank, will be covered for the next month with a glorious mixture of flowers and ferns.

Sycamores and silver maples grow along the stranded old creek beds, where the creek has changed its course many times over hundreds of years.

This 55-acre property has been essentially undisturbed since early pioneer times and had remained in one family's possession for over 117 years. It is noted for the astonishing number of tree species found in the floodplain and higher ground bordering the creek—half the trees native to Michigan, making it truly a "natural aboretum." There are uncommon varieties such as those shown plus hackberry, honeylocust, chinquapin oak, cork elm, black maple, wafer ash, and pawpaw. The Powell sanctuary is good for hiking, birding, and animal study.

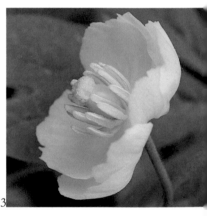

1 *Grazed vs. ungrazed woods at edge of Kope Kon Nature Sanctuary, Branch County. A stout livestock-proof fence protects the groundcover on the sanctuary side.*

2 *The red-bellied woodpecker is found here and in several other MNA woodlands in southern Michigan.*

3 *Closeup of the may-apple flower, which hides beneath the plant's large umbrella-like leaves shown in 1.*

4 *The nearby Adeline Kershaw Woods Sanctuary is a mature* **oak-hickory** *stand. This is the familiar shagbark hickory.*

5 *The kingnut hickory, Carya laciniosa (SC), bears unusually large nuts prized for making cakes and cookies. This is the only hickory that has orange-colored winter twigs.*

Southwest Michigan North to Mackinac

Prairie remnants, sand dunes, and rare "disjunct species," normally found only in states further south, are among the singular features of western Michigan protected in MNA sanctuaries. The 46 counties of this section of the Lower Peninsula shown on the map have less than one-fourth of Michigan's population. In these are 37 MNA sanctuaries of which 19 are in the southern seven counties located along the Chicago-Detroit corridor which, it is predicted, will one day be solidly developed.

In southwest Michigan, travel can be on lovely tree-lined roads where you pass by gracious homes and well-tended orchards that delight the eye. Quaint events such as antique fairs, the "blessing of the blossoms" in fruit belt country, occasional plowing by horses, and tours of vineyards, all contribute to the oldtime feeling of the stability of life as it was fifty years ago.

"Going north" from the southeast part of the state means via I-75; from the southwest, it is by way of US-131. Starting at Newaygo County, you will get the feeling of actually entering the north country. From Clare County on, the smell of sweet fern permeates the air, and sandy soils and evergreens take over. From this latitude every county, from the shore of Lake Michigan to the lesser traveled and lesser known shore of Lake Huron, is Michigan's playground for all-season recreational living.

In botanical terms, a "tension zone" lying between Muskegon and Bay City also marks a division between plants of southern and northern types.

The upper counties were burned in the days of the forest fires that followed extensive logging in the 1880's, reducing them to scarred ruins. Reforestation has now healed many wounds, and, to the casual viewer, the pine woods again look in fine condition.

What is a Natural Area?

In making choices of locations to preserve, the MNA has tried, wherever possible, to concentrate its efforts on land that is still in the same state as when Michigan was first settled. Such a property can be termed a "natural area." Large or small, it retains its pristine character, especially the undisturbed ground cover. Native plants persist there in their original environment, which frequently harbors unusual flora that have been destroyed elsewhere. While lands of this description still exist—usually because of some quirk of topography—they are very difficult to find. Owning them outright is the best way to insure that they remain unchanged for future generations to enjoy.

What is a Native Habitat?

There are no published lists of habitats in Michigan, although several proposed drafts have been drawn up by the Michigan Natural Features Inventory. A habitat is a natural ecosystem which has developed without human interference. For example, if nature alone runs its course, in a climax after hundreds of years, the forests of Michigan will reach one of twelve kinds outlined in this book. This might be **oak-hickory** and, eventually, **beech-maple**. On rock, along shoreline, **bedrock beach** habitat may form; wetlands will develop into **marsh, wet meadow,** etc., with flora adapted perfectly to each situation.

We show you roughly two-thirds of Michigan's habitats (see Index, page 100). *Curtis' Vegetation of Wisconsin*, which describes habitats quite similar to Michigan's, is a good book to consult. See Appendix, page 97.

The MNA Concept of Nature Preservation

The MNA holds to a policy of non-intervention, even after natural catastrophes. Below is the scene today at Green River Nature Sanctuary (page 49) showing one section where first, beavers created a large dam which killed many cedars. Later, the dead trees were laid sideways by hurricane force winds. They may persist "as is" for centuries since white cedar is very resistant to decay. Likewise, the Leaning Giant of the Estivants (page 82) is left at its resting place along the Montreal River in the Keweenaw, to rot down eventually and create new humus for other trees to grow.

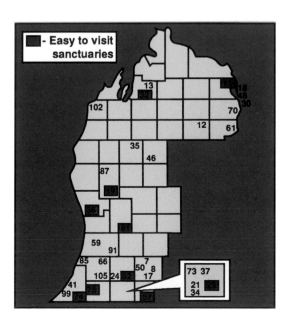

1

Dowagiac Woods
Nature Sanctuary

Called the "jewel in the crown" of MNA properties, this preserve can satisfy many nature interests. Photographers focus on wildflowers. Hikers investigate the preserve's far corners. Woods lovers can study both swamp and beech-maple forests. Bird watchers can find 49 different species of nesting birds. Neophyte city-dwellers can enjoy the wild along easy, well-marked trails.

Flower seekers need go no farther than the 300-foot loop trail that starts at the roadside ditch at the entrance (5-p.32). "I've only been here five minutes and I've already seen 22 kinds of wildflowers," exclaimed Judy Clark, a visitor from Pennsylvania, on May 2, 1988. An hour's hunt in this area during the peak blooming period in April and early May can result in a list of 50 species. A top attraction here is the blue-eyed Mary, *Collinsia verna* (1), which also grows in other damp parts of the woods, blooming for six weeks starting April 1. Its dainty flowers, with two blue and two white petals, make a cheerful contrast to other spring species like the white trillium. At the height of the season, a one-square-foot section of Dowagiac yielded a count of 86 individual plants of nine different species.

For those to whom nature means "forest," Dowagiac offers 150 wooded acres with 45 species, including lofty tulip poplars (3) and such unusual trees as the black ash, chinquapin oak, cork elm, and the rare kingnut hickory (SC). Spicebush and pawpaw dominate acres of mushy ground.

Tale of the Skink

On September 6, 1987, MNA photographers John Sohlden and Kernie King were walking down Frost Road when they glimpsed a most unexpected sight. Kernie recalls: "John saw it first—the flash of a blue tail disappearing into a hole. While I dug away the earth cover, John captured the creature with a quick grab as it tried to make its getaway. It was Michigan's only native lizard, the five-lined skink, *Eumeces fasciatus*. I took our drinking water and rinsed off John's hand, then the skink, and made the photo (2). After we lowered the skink to earth, unharmed, it quickly darted off.

This species has an unusual defense mechanism. If the skink is caught by the tail, the tail breaks off and the skink escapes. Soon a new tail will grow. *Eumeces fasciatus* has been seen several times at Dowagiac Woods and seems to be reproducing, since the one we saw was a juvenile, as indicated by its brilliant blue tail."

2

3   4

4 *"The year's at the spring, and day's at the morn,"* and a young admirer smiles at a sunlit blossom of the large-flowering white trillium, the showiest member of this family of native lilies.

5

6

6 *The zebra swallowtail ranges across the eastern United States, wherever its host plant, the pawpaw, grows. Field marks are the bold black stripes on its light gray wings, the long sword-like tail, the scarlet spot on its lower back, and sapphire dots at the base of its wings.*

Dowagiac Woods (continued)

An unnamed tributary (8) of the Dowagiac River flows through the woods, slow-moving and clear, fed by numerous springs and streams. In some stretches, the stream is bordered with muck; in others, it is easy to walk on the sandy bottom.

Birders can watch dozens of woodland inhabitants. Woodpeckers, black-capped chickadees, and ruffed grouse stay year round. Summer residents include woodcock, wood duck, scarlet tanager, wood thrush, rose-breasted grosbeak, indigo bunting, and Acadian flycatcher. The common yellowthroat warbler frequents damp, open places—the yellow warbler, shrubby areas.

The Woods is also a haven for several plants and animals in danger of becoming extinct in Michigan. Threatened are the *Poa paludigena*, or marsh blue grass, the Greek valerian, the black rat snake, and the Eastern box turtle; of Special Concern include the kingnut hickory, the spotted turtle, and a snail, *Fontigens nicklineana*. The Dowagiac Woods' great size is a major factor in the survival of these species here. They need the space and peaceful solitude of an extensive untouched area to continue their age-old patterns of survival. Another interesting plant is the inconspicuous spring ephemeral, the tiny false mermaid, *Floerkea proseripinacoides*.

Three delighted onlookers (5) view beds of blue-eyed Mary near the southwest corner of Dowagiac Woods. Trees here include Ohio buckeye (right), blue beech, sugar maple, and willow (left, with catkins). The twisted rope-like stems in back of the figures are wild grape vines.

Bertha Daubendiek reminisces, "It was my privilege in 1981, as we were studying the woods before acquisition, to visit it every weekend for six weeks from the last of March through the first of May. It was an exciting and uplifting experience I have never forgotten. At first a green fuzz appeared everywhere on the ground. Somewhere else, this would have turned into grass, but it soon became apparent that at Dowagiac Woods every tuft of green was topped by a wildflower bud. The progression was slow but steady, until everywhere there were flowers, all jammed together. Some other woods have two peaks of bloom, in April and in the middle of May. But not at Dowagiac. No matter what day you go in that six weeks' period, blooms are everywhere."

The MNA completed fund raising to purchase this fabulous nature property on January 3, 1983. Its 220 acres in Cass County are the largest moist, virgin soil woodland left in Michigan today. Never plowed, planted or grazed, it retains all of its original natural diversity. It is a living example of how the forests looked when the first settlers came.

If you can make a spring visit to only one MNA preserve, make it this one!

7 *The black rat snake (T) is harmless to humans. This one, still lethargic from winter hibernation, stretches out on a maple branch to warm itself in the April sun, allowing Norma Ludecke to take its portrait. This snake is an agile climber. It eats anything from small mammals and lizards to birds and eggs. Mating in both spring and fall, it produces a clutch of 5-30 eggs. It is normally active in the daytime but becomes nocturnal in the heat of summer.*

7

8

9 *The American bladdernut grows in thickets on floodplains or river banks in the south half of the Lower Peninsula. At Dowagiac it is visible from Frost Road. The fruits which mature in late summer, have puffed-up papery capsules that pop when squeezed; the seeds rattle when dry.*

9

Prairies of Southwest Michigan

In 1963, a marly wet prairie tract at Lakeville Swamp with a large sedge fen was MNA's first location for prairie blazing stars and tall turkeyfoot grass. In 1969 Newaygo Prairie Nature Sanctuary was acquired. Now there are 21 refugia of rare grasslands in the program, where many little-known plants too rare to appear in general wildflower guides can be found.

Prairies are heirlooms of Michigan's original landscape, most of them in the southwestern counties as far north as Newaygo County.

Only remnants of the prairie remain because these lands were most easily turned into agricultural land. In Michigan, a state originally over 95% forested, prairie amounted to only about 100,000 acres (0.3%) of a total land area of 36,450,000 acres. Especially in the southwest part of the state, in the lowest tiers of counties, names of many towns, roads, and streams signify a prairie origin.

A true prairie is composed of more than 50% native grasses. Scattered among them are colorful flowering plants, called forbs. The prairie world is a secret, fragile one with diverse treasures to be found through the seasons. Flowers and grasses are abundant in late summer, with one-fourth blooming after August 15. In early spring, the buds of tiny buttercups, bird's foot violets, and cleft phlox peek an inch or two above the cold spring soil, followed closely by the slightly taller puccoon, lupine, and thimbleweed. Next, taller and taller plants appear until finally big bluestem, Indian grass, sunflowers, goldenrods and asters take center stage. Many are of the composite, legume, and figwort families.

Prairies are incredibly diverse and each has plants suited to its particular soil conditions. Some are lush, as at Sauk (p. 37), and some constantly struggle with drought as at Newaygo and Sand Prairie.

(6) is a view of the 110 acre Newaygo Prairie Nature Sanctuary. Newaygo is a champion of Michigan prairies, visited by people from all parts of southern Michigan. Woods bordering the prairie bowl are red oak, white oak, and white pine. Established in the bowl are wild black cherry and the Allegheny or sloe plum, *Prunus alleghaniensis,* var. *davisii* (SC). At this outstanding example of **dry sand prairie**, you can see a large stand of needle grass, *Stipa spartea,* alongside the road (foreground). It blooms in mid-May and has an inch-long, sharp-pointed seed with a five inch tail that twists itself into the ground like a corkscrew. Over 100 species grow on this prairie on Sparta loamy sand. Rare plants here include western silvery aster, *Aster sericeus* (T), and the prairie bird's foot violet, *Viola pedatifida* (T).

Bird life at Newaygo Prairie ranges from bluebirds and prairie warblers in the open spaces to whip-poor-wills at the wood's edge.

1

2

3

34

4

1 *The white blue-eyed grass,* Sisyrinchium albidum, *blooms in late April beside the trail at Goose Creek Grasslands.*

2 *Indian grass,* Sorghastrum nutans, *(see text).*

3 *Prickly pear cactus,* Opuntia humifusa, *is found at Newaygo Prairie and blooms July 4.*

4 *Prairie smoke,* Geum triflorum *('1'), also at Newaygo, blooms May through June.*

5 *Eight foot tall big bluestem grass, part of a two-acre stand, with reddish tops visible from Commerce Road at Yntema Wildlife Oasis, Oakland County. Wait until September to look here for it.*

5

6

7

8

A half-dozen milkweed species are found on prairies and all attract butterflies.
7 *shows the spindle-shaped seed pods of butterfly-weed,* Asclepias tuberosa.
8 *shows the coral hairstreak butterfly,* Harkenclenus titus, *on butterfly-weed.*
9 *big bluestem,* Andropogon gerardii, *is the most important Michigan tall grass and is also called turkeyfoot grass, from its resemblance to the foot of a big bird. It does not appear above ground until mid-August, when it pushes up rapidly and flowers profusely in September and October. It can be easily found and learned at Goose Creek Grasslands Nature Sanctuary and several others.*

10

How to Learn the Prairie Grasses

Enhance your enjoyment of prairies by learning some of the grasses and forbs. Few books offer help. Sticking close to a scheduled field trip leader and making notes will bring rewards.

There are only 17 grasses of major interest. Of the eight shown in this book you can easily locate six in your first year. Then go on to the others. Start by visiting Newaygo Prairie in May to see needle grass in bloom, and in June to see the seed twist its way out. In late July, five-foot-tall Indian grass comes into glory. Third most important and easiest-to-learn grass, it will be found on the short trail at Goose Creek. By running your hand over the unforgettably soft and silky seed head, you will always be able to distinguish it from other grasses.

Big bluestem is also easy—its height and distinctive head give it away. Remember, all grasses have flowers that last about 10 days, the same as other blooming plants. Switch grass can be learned at Five Lakes Muskegon, Newaygo or Barvicks. It is the first thing you see upon the open sand dunes. Add an October visit to Newaygo for little bluestem and you will have mastered four common grasses plus needle grass. A trip to Goose Creek Grasslands to learn the rare *Sporobolus heterolepis,* page 68, should be the basis for your second year study.

Michiganders can share the feeling of the pioneers when walking in thick shoulder-high prairie grasses on MNA preserves.

10 *September dawn at Sauk Indian Trail Prairie Plant Preserve along the old Chicago Road (US-12) in southern St. Joseph County. Naturalists Edna Newnan (left) and Vicki Nuzzo, prairie expert from Illinois, examine a stalk of swamp milkweed. Its silvery bark fibers are used by dozens of bird species to construct nests.*

Sauk is a long, narrow quarter-acre wedge of **mesic black soil prairie,** *miraculously never plowed, lying between US-12 and the oldest railroad bed in the region. Prairie ground cover here includes prairie coreopsis, Coreopsis palmata (T), lead plant, Amorpha canescens, (T), and dwarf chinquapin oak, a shrub bearing full-size acorns.*

11 *Second in importance of the grasses is little bluestem grass,* Andropogon scoparius, *last to bloom (mid-October), which prefers sandy soil in a dry prairie. Up to three feet high, it is profuse at the north part of Newaygo Prairie and at Sand Prairie Preserve.*

11

1

2

3

4

5　6

Southwest Michigan Specialties

1 The unusual green violet, *Hybanthus concolor* (SC), blooms in mid-May at Kope Kon Nature Sanctuary, Branch County. At first glance it is not easy to recognize as a violet, though its structure is typical of the family. In late summer the big flattened seeds are distinctive.

2 Pink lady-slipper or moccasin-flower, *Cypripedium acaule,* is one of the larger native orchids. At Fish Lake Bog it blooms the week before Memorial Day along the edges of the quaking bog, on low hummocks under the tamarack trees.

3 The Eastern box turtle, *Terrapena carolina,* a "land turtle," is found in only 17 counties of southwest Michigan, inhabiting moist open woods. This tame species frequently lives to be over 60 years old and feeds on mushrooms, insects and larvae, earthworms, and various fruits.

4 Wulfenia or kittentails, *Besseya bullii* (E-USA, T), is protected at the Fitch Plant Preserve in St. Joseph County, where it grows on a dry steep bank.

5 The rose-pink, or bitterbloom (T), is a member of the gentian family. It flowers in late August at Pepperidge Dunes Plant Preserve in Berrien County. The species name, *Sabatia angularis,* refers to the sharply four-angled stem.

6 The graceful Virginia bluebells, *Mertensia virginica* (T), is a native plant of open woods and lowlands. The first two weeks of May its nodding clusters of trumpet-shaped blooms decorate the floodplain along the Coldwater River with patches of blue; (the pink buds gradually change color as they mature). A two-acre, non-development conservation easement protects this plant in Bowne Township, Kent County.

1

2

3

Trillium Ravine Plant Preserve

This area is a classic **beech-maple** *woods (1). In the picture, the grey-barked trees are American beech; at center is a sugar maple. In this choice habitat grow two species of toad trilliums (T), whose range barely extends into southern Michigan. The upper plant in the picture (3) is the toadshade, Trillium sessile; the lower plant is the prairie trillium, T. recurvatum. Notice that the stalkless flowers rest directly on the leaves which are mottled like the skin of a toad. Wood poppy, Stylophorum diphyllum (2), occurs only in Michigan's southwestern counties. (Do not confuse it with the European celandine.)*

Pennfield Bog Plant Preserve

Located seven miles northeast of Battle Creek in Calhoun County, this 25 acre area presents the vegetative transition from high dry woods to the open water of Little Goose Lake. The preserve is classified "C," requiring an experienced guide, because the **bog** is dangerous and separated from the dry ground by a dense thicket of shrubs.

Of a field trip August 10, 1980, led by long-time MNA member Rita Juckett, Lyle Rizor recalls, "We approached the bog through a red maple woods on a gentle slope to the lake level. We waded through shallow water past a bed of calla lilies and penetrated the thicket composed of highbush blueberry, dogwood, Michigan holly, willow, poison sumac, and tamaracks of varying maturity. Underfoot was a spongy mat of roots, leatherleaf, and sphagnum moss. In places this mat moved under our weight, indicating that it was a 'quaking bog' floating on water. Among the tamaracks we found cattails and water-horehound."

This bog's specialty is the yellow fringed orchis, *Platanthera* or *Habenaria ciliaris* (T) (1), with a cluster of yellow-orange florets atop a stem one to two feet tall. In the picture (2) the larger white dots at left are cottongrass, and the snow-like flecks are white beak rush. Another bog specialty is the Virginia chain fern. Pitcher plants, two kinds of sundew, rare bog rosemary, and rose pogonia, *Isotria verticillata* (T), can also be found during visits earlier in the year.

More about Trillium Ravine

We highly recommend visiting this preserve in Berrien County, about a six mile drive from Niles' city limits. The access is easy, and the open park-like character of the beech-maple forest with its widely spaced large trees makes a delightful setting for a leisurely walk. Other common tree species growing here are basswood, ironwood and red oak. The toad trilliums bloom early—one variety beginning approximately April 9 and the other about one week later, lasting about two weeks. By May 1, this area is like Dowagiac Woods—it is hard to find a place to walk without stepping on flowers—so it is best to stay on the trail. The floral carpet features large-flowered trillium, false rue-anemone, may-apple, yellow trout-lily, and Canada and wooly blue violet.

1

2

Five Lakes Muskegon Sanctuary

This area of 53.2 acres in the outskirts of Muskegon has been known since 1900 for the quantities of rare plants discovered there. It is a botanical Sherlock Holmes' paradise. The Michigan Natural Features Inventory rates it as having the highest number of "at risk species" (2-E, 4-T, 6-SC) of any preserve in the state. It is also an agreeable place to visit despite being situated near an industrial area. From Evanston Road the entrance walk leads through a peaceful grove of young oaks for 600 feet then opens out on the expansive **coastal plain marsh** (1)—a special type of wetland that is flooded in spring and virtually dries up in summer. There are four zones shown in the picture: the driest zone, in the foreground, is composed of mesic sand grasses; the dark zone, of twig rushes, spike rushes, and some rare sedges; the light zone near the water, of cattails and blue-joint grass; at water's edge are floating and emergent-leaved aquatic plants.

In the original Federal Survey of the region in 1836, the entire area was shown as one large body of water. In recent years however it shrank into smaller ponds locally called the "Five Lakes."

As the water receded, the sandy soil filled in with extraordinary native plants—most are those called "coastal plains disjuncts," as well as prairie species. The first category refers to plants whose normal range is along the Atlantic seacoast but which also grow near the east shore of Lake Michigan with no intermediary colonies. Meadow beauty, *Rhexia virginica* (SC) (2), is associated with these species, flowering in open marshy areas along the lakeshore. In late August, its deep rosy petals and yellow anthers are a pleasure to behold.

A sedge, *Scirpus hallii* (E), is also found here as well as an uncommon form of blue-eyed grass. In summer, orange puccoon, bird's foot violet, and lupine brighten the meadows, followed by prairie plants such as blazing stars and dozens of rare grasses, sedges, and bulrushes. Wildlife includes the hognosed snake, a variety of ducks and wading birds, and the marsh hawk.

One of the highlights of visiting here is to listen to the melodious warbling of bluebirds which nest in tree cavities at the wood's edge.

Michigan's 83 Native Trees

Michigan is a forest state and the study of its trees can be pursued easily as a do-it-yourself hobby. You can start by carrying guides with pictures to match flower, leaf, bark, and fruit. The bewildering variety can be mastered by identifying a few field marks.

It is important to learn the botanical name of each tree, because many have several common names. For example, *Nyssa sylvatica*, p.46, is known by different sources as black gum, pepperidge, tupelo, black tupelo, and sour-gum.

Different books also disagree on the break-off point between a shrub and a small tree. Our list of 83 excludes eight that our botanist classed as shrubs: speckled alder, Canada plum, Douglas haw, p.74; green alder, p. 78; witch hazel, p. 46; dwarf chinquapin oak, p. 37; Allegheny or sloe plum, p. 34, and the American or wild plum, p. 13.

One advantage of tree study is that a tree is stationary; it can be located and checked at various times of the year. After familiarizing yourself with the common cultivated varieties, you can concentrate on native trees at MNA sanctuaries, where samples of all of Michigan's 83 indigenous species may be found.

Two things will simplify your study. First, you can learn a third of the 83 by paying attention to the families of native maples (seven), hickories (four), elms (three), oaks (twelve), and ash (four). Second, you can study the state-wide tree distribution and apply yourself to identifying those in your region:

27 found throughout the state: *basswood, tamarack, white pine, jack pine, red pine, hemlock, white cedar, sugar maple, red maple, largetooth aspen, quaking aspen, yellow birch, tall juneberry, smooth juneberry, white birch, pin cherry, hop-hornbeam or ironwood, choke cherry, pagoda tree, American elm, American beech, red oak, white ash, black ash, red ash, smooth sumac, and staghorn sumac;* 33 abundant only in the south half of the LP: *flowering dogwood, pepperidge, red cedar, sassafras, tulip poplar, cottonwood, black willow, peach-leaf willow, wild sweet crab, hawthorn, black maple, silver maple, boxelder, pignut hickory, shagbark hickory, black walnut, wild black cherry, American hornbeam or blue beach, hackberry, white oak, swamp white oak, bur oak, chinquapin oak, black oak, scarlet oak, pin oak, sycamore, rock elm, slippery elm, poison sumac, wafer ash, bladdernut, and prickly ash;* only eight trees abundant in the UP and northern LP: *balsam fir, black spruce, white spruce, balsam poplar, mountain maple, striped maple, American mountain ash, and showy mountain ash;* with special distribution: *butternut, rare in LP and in two counties of UP; bitternut hickory; nannyberry, frequent LP and locally frequent east part of UP from Houghton County.*

Another dozen trees considered unusual or rare that deserve reading about are found only in the southernmost counties: pawpaw, honeylocust, American chestnut, and redbud, all on p. 44; blue ash, p. 27; black cottonwood and Kentucky coffeetree, this page; Ohio buckeye, p. 26; kingnut hickory, p. 28; also dwarf hackberry, red mulberry, and shingle oak.

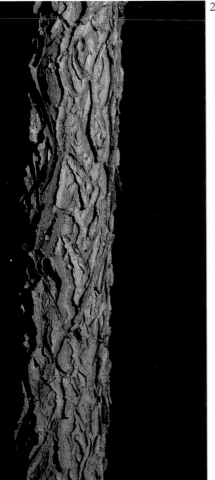

Pictured here are two of Michigan's rarest trees. (1) shows bark of the black cottonwood (T) and leaf (right side)— which is as big as a man's hand—contrasted with a leaf of the common cottonwood. To see this unusual species you must make a pilgrimage to the MNA Black Cottonwood Preserve near Vicksburg, Kalamazoo County (see map pages 92-93). Another easy tree to find is the Kentucky coffeetree (SC). (2) shows the bark photographed at the Virginia Bluebells Preserve near the Coldwater River in southeast Kent County. A coffeetree grove can also be seen along the road at Kope Kon. The bipinnately compound four-foot-long leaf (3) is being held by a small boy of about the same length.

4

5

6

4 The American chestnut is prized for its edible sweet nuts. Here they are shown still in their prickly bur casings and with catkins attached. The stately "spreading chestnut tree" held a commanding position in the rich forests of the northeastern United States until the species was virtually wiped out by the Asiatic chestnut blight in the early part of the 20th century. MNA's small stand in Allegan County seems resistant to the disease.

5 Blossoms of the redbud emerge directly along the branches, coming out before the large heart-shaped leaves. At White Pigeon River Sanctuary, near Indiana, they appear about May 1. The seeds are packed in long pea-like pods. A tree of bottomlands, the redbud's natural range is only in the southern tier of counties.

6 The honeylocust has needle-sharp branched thorns on its trunk and branches. It can be found at Bean\Creek, White Pigeon River, and Dowagiac Woods.

7 The exotic maroon blossom of the pawpaw tree appears in late May and June. This small tree, not over 10 feet high, bears edible fruit which looks like a small banana and smells like one, too. It should be eaten when fully ripe and starting to blacken, but many birds and mammals eat it green. There are nice groves of pawpaw at Powell Memorial and Dowagiac Woods.

7

9

8

10

8 & 9 *The pure white "petals" of flowering dogwood are actually bracts surrounding the small dense cluster of greenish flowerlets. The crimson drupe is eagerly eaten by over 86 kinds of birds, not to mention squirrels. The graceful dogwood, a small tree of the understory, thrives in the rich soils of southern Michigan. See it in bloom around Mother's Day at both sides of the parking area at Dowagiac Woods. It is also prolific at Columbia Nature Sanctuary, Jackson County, and at Wade Memorial, Allegan County, where it comes into glory a week or so later, due to the "lake influence" of Lake Michigan.*

10 *Catkins of the chinquapin oak bear tiny yellow flowers that are wind pollinated. This photo was taken at Woodruff Creek Preserve, Livingston County. The tree also grows at Bean Creek and Dowagiac Woods.*

11 *The fruit of the bitternut hickory is so acrid that it is not fit for human consumption, but the wood, when burned, gives meats a true hickory smoked flavor.*

12 *Delicate blooms of the wild sweet crab can be found in May along the entrance to Brennan Sanctuary. The crab's small green apples make good jelly. Individual trees bloom every other year.*

11

12

1

2

3

Algird Barvicks Sand Dunes Nature Sanctuary

This 40-acre **open sand dunes** habitat (4) is located in Van Buren County, a mile inland from Lake Michigan. An old dune blowout is surrounded by a mature, mixed species woods of maple, tulip, black oak, hemlock, and yellow birch trees. A shallow depression at the west end of the blowout has developed into a **coastal plain marsh** (barely visible in center of picture) containing disjunct plant species. The edge of the open dune area is being stabilized by stands of oak, witch-hazel, pin and sand cherry, and sassafras. There are black tupelo trees, *Nyssa sylvatica* (3), also called black gum or pepperidge trees, up to 30 feet tall. The first tree to show color in fall, its dark green leathery leaves change to brilliant shades of crimson after Labor Day.

This preserve contains 12 plant species that do not occur on other MNA lands. Four of the 12 have Threatened status: a three-awned grass, *Aristida necopina,* a sedge, *Carex seorsa,* a rush, *Juncus scirpoides,* and the clubmoss *Lycopodium adpressum.*

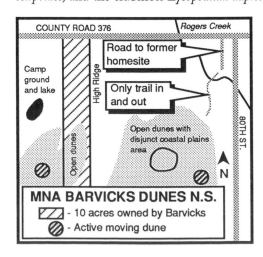

COUNTY ROAD 376 — Rogers Creek

Road to former homesite

Camp ground and lake

High Ridge

Only trail in and out

Open dunes

80TH ST.

Open dunes with disjunct coastal plains area

N

MNA BARVICKS DUNES N.S.

⧄ - 10 acres owned by Barvicks

⊘ - Active moving dune

4

1 *Black tupelo male and female flowers of June produce a ½ inch long fruit which turns blue-black in October.*

2 & 5 *are switch grass,* Panicum virgatum. *Along with little bluestem grass, dune grass, hoary puccoon, and wormwood, it typifies the vegetation growing on the dry sandy soil.*

4 *Sassafras attains shrub size in dry sand but can grow to be a 40 to 50 foot tree in moist woods.*

6 *Its fruits are borne on bright red club-shaped stalks. The leaves are a novel feature because they come in three different shapes—oval, one-, and two-lobed—all on a single plant. They turn fiery orange in autumn, looking like a bonfire on the landscape.*

Barvicks is a B/C class sanctuary requiring a guide.

5

6

1 *At Lost Lake, adventurers Alice and Bill Gosline and Larry Kastler family, on an MNA field trip bushwhack through the* **rich conifer swamp.** *The white cedars fall naturally due to wind and weak roots, making openings where shrubs and wildflowers can grow.*

2 *Grass-of-Parnassus is one of the blossoms that brighten the lake border.*

3 *Black spruce and tamarack encircle the rush and sedge mat of Lost Lake, a* **northern wet meadow.**

2

1

3

Lost Lake Nature Sanctuary

The three north country sanctuaries mentioned on these pages represent a contrast between two hard-to-find sanctuaries and an easy one.

You can expect to be well rewarded for time and effort expended to explore Lost Lake. From the road, walk west by compass to the cedar swamp, and proceed through a tangle of moss-covered logs, bog rosemary, and giant ferns. Inside half an hour you should encounter your first view of Lost Lake. Its shallow, reedy shoreline is bordered mainly by open marshland surrounded by an unbroken stand of black spruce, white cedar, and alder trees.

Pitcher plants, orchids, grass-of-Parnassus, and sundews may be found in the quaking bog that extends north from the lake. This classic **northern wet meadow** habitat, pictured in the foreground of (3), contains open bog plants among the sedges, with black spruce predominant along its margin. Acidic in nature, this type of habitat exhibits less floral diversity than its often alkaline southern counterpart.

Green River Nature Sanctuary

This 40 acres in Antrim County is another untamed preserve. Flowing through it is a quarter mile of "the Prize of the North"—a pure crystal trout stream crisscrossed with fallen logs from white cedars crowding its banks (4). The logs hardly decay under the cold water and some are thought to be over a century old. The brook trout is the renowned native game fish of the river, where chill temperature and gravelly beds provide ideal spawning conditions. Northern plants such as white camas, wood lily, and Indian paintbrush flourish in the area, while under the cedars, both downy and creeping rattlesnake plantain orchids can be found.

Cedar River Nature Sanctuary

Located eight miles from the Green River Preserve, the Cedar is also located in picturesque Antrim County, popularly known as the "Black Hills of Michigan." It is an easy-to-visit favorite—just drive north of Mancelona on West Limits Road three miles and turn left on Doerr Road. After 1¼ miles, the preserve is on both sides of the river south of the road. You can follow fishermen's paths along the quarter mile of riverfront to explore the cedar swamp. A ⅛ - mile drive west of the bridge will bring you to upland deciduous woods—a choice spot for spring wildflowers.

4

5

5 *This is a place where the range of the two varieties of spring beauty overlap. The northern type, Claytonia caroliniana (right) has a more erect habit and broader leaves than the southern C. virginica (left). Here both plants grow side-by-side.*

The Miracle of Bird Life

Birds brighten our lives. A "silent spring" would portend the death of our world; we must never let it happen. Ninety percent of all the kinds of birds that normally nest in Michigan live on MNA preserves in ideal territory for breeding and food supply.

Bird study is the most usual way in which people become interested in the outdoor world, learning first the permanent residents—the ones that do not roam much and nest where they stay the year around. These are familiar species such as the woodpeckers, tufted titmouse, owls, goldfinch, cardinal, ruffed grouse, white-breasted nuthatch, bluejay, and chickadee. About 150 kinds of summer residents swell the nesting population, arriving in stages. The hardiest come in March and April and stay latest in the fall. Warblers and other warm weather birds appear in May and leave by July and August. Others are migrants that only pass through Michigan. Though these are interesting, the MNA program is focused seriously on preserving habitat for birds that stay to breed.

Does the MNA program provide such situations for all the 188 regularly nesting species? (Forty-four other kinds have only been observed to nest once or twice in the state.) In 1977, and again in 1987, the MNA conducted a census of its largest sanctuaries to learn the answer. The final count was 170. Of the 18 kinds lacking, most are birds of the open countryside. The MNA is currently seeking to add proper nesting grounds for them as well. What inner trigger causes birds to return annually from some far-off wintering ground to their same preferred home breeding territory is one of the great mysteries of nature.

Within a single preserve, the 245-acre Estivant Pines Nature Sanctuary at the tip of the Keweenaw, an astonishing number of 82 species were found nesting. Some interesting ones are: broad-winged and sharp-shinned hawk, barred and northern saw-whet owl, yellow-bellied sapsucker, pileated woodpecker, olive-sided and yellow-bellied flycatcher, raven, red-breasted nuthatch, brown creeper, golden-crowned and ruby-crowned kinglet, solitary and Philadelphia vireo, rare northern woods warblers, and red and white-winged crossbills. Other super MNA birding spots to visit in early summer are: White Pigeon River, Timberland, Dowagiac Woods, Kope Kon, and Goose Creek Grasslands.

1

2

3 The Caspian tern (T) needs isolation from human disturbance to reproduce successfully. At left, a male presents a minnow to the lone nestling tucked beneath the female's wing. Adult Caspians are similar to the herring gull in size and behavior.

4 One of MNA's three Wilderness Islands (below), with a beach of gleaming white limestone cobbles rising 11 feet above the surface of Lake Michigan, provides an ideal nesting habitat and is now the site of the largest Caspian colony in the Great Lakes region, with 365-605 nests annually. John Sohlden experienced the thrill of standing among hundreds of the terns with their blood-red bills when he visited the colony by boat in 1987 to catch this parade of Caspians on the island's pebbled shore.

3

4

5

1 On capturing the eagle picture, Kernie King writes, "Of several photography trips for the MNA, the one I enjoyed the most was June 27, 1987, at the Lake Superior Nature Sanctuary, to seek out the bald eagle. I slowly crept along the edge of an alder thicket to reach a spot that would give me a clear view of the nest and still remain concealed—but I was not careful enough. One adult was on the nest and flew away with a loud scream as I approached. I proceeded on and got into position in case the eagle came back. After a short wait the mate flew in and landed on the nest, not knowing I was there. I made one exposure and, while refocusing, the eagle spotted my movement and flew away. From then on it was like playing a game as the eagles took turns flying in and landing on a branch. I would take a picture, and they would fly away again."

2 The MNA owns three bird nesting islands in Lake Huron's Thunder Bay—Grass Island, Bird Island, and Gull Island (on left), which was the first one to be acquired by the organization in 1969. Its 12 acres provide nesting habitat for herring gulls, ducks, Canada geese, black-crowned night herons and great blues. To visit it is an unforgettable experience. As you walk around the edge of the island, the gulls you approach rise up and scream and squawk furiously as you pass by, then settle down again peacefully with their young. It takes an hour to slowly encircle the island. Any longer visit is not recommended for fear of disrupting the birds nesting activities.

5 The black-capped chickadee came out ahead in the bird census as the friendliest bird—it flew to greet us every time. It was also, along with the robin, the most plentiful, being present at every MNA preserve.

1 *Bob Rogers of Alpena, caretaker of the Peter Sanctuary, studies the "Natural Beauty Road" sign at Hamilton Road, first road to be given this designation based on a law proposed by the Michigan Nature Association in 1970. The Natural Beauty Road Act allows citizens to petition their county to preserve a specific portion of roadway in its natural state, restricting any alteration of its vegetation or features without a prior public hearing. Michigan now has more than 900 miles of Natural Beauty Roads.*

2 *Dwarf lake iris, Iris lacustris (T), is a small (five inches tall), endemic plant growing around the shores of Lake Huron and Lake Michigan in only a few counties, mostly near the Straits. To see the iris and also the bird's-eye primrose are the "must" reasons to go to the Peter preserve. Dwarf lake iris will be at its peak Memorial Day, but its blossoms can be found in shady spots up to three weeks thereafter. For the primrose, go about May 23rd and look in wet edges along the lakeshore.*

3

4

Julius C. and Marie Moran Peter
Memorial Nature Sanctuary (formerly Grass Lake)

This northern wilderness area of 95 acres is located half an hour's drive from the city of Alpena. Access to the preserve is by way of a trail running about a quarter of a mile north off Hamilton Road, which leads to a clearing on the southwest shore of Grass Lake.

Visitors walking here may observe many striking flower species: ram's head orchid and two varieties of yellow lady-slipper, pink and one-sided pyrola, twinflower, fringed polygala, wood lily, buffalo berry, and spurred and fringed gentian. Trailing arbutus (3)—for many, a favorite wildflower of the northern woods—can also be found here. This evergreen plant bears sweet-scented pearly pink blossoms in early spring.

The path is also a good location for bird watchers to listen for and observe hawks, warblers, rose-breasted grosbeaks, Wilson's snipe, and pileated woodpeckers. If you stand quietly at the lake's edge you may see many of the numerous species of waterfowl and wading birds that are attracted to these remote waters.

From the moment you step out of your car you will see the three-inch high spears of dwarf lake iris, a species that carpets all the trails in small openings throughout the preserve. At a marked trail junction, take the left fork which leads to the southwest corner of the sanctuary, where a side road heads south to Hamilton Road.

For a truly memorable wilderness interlude, a visitor with a compass (don't go without one) and preserve map and at least three hours to spare, can take a much more challenging unmarked route. Take the right fork north through the woods from the junction. You will reach the lakeshore near the northern border of the preserve. Return along the shoreline for about a mile to reach the clearing and the trail back to Hamilton Road. This route takes you to lake edges where seaside arrow grass (5), duck potato, water weed, rushes and sedges grow.

The primeval character of this area was confirmed by the finding of bear tracks and droppings during the MNA explorations at the time of acquisition. The black bear is a shy and secretive animal which requires a large secluded region in which to forage for food.

Signs of the presence of deer, raccoon, and snowshoe hare are plentiful. The porcupine (4) is also a resident of the forest. Slow moving and dimwitted, it depends upon the barbed quills on its back and tail for protection from natural enemies. Spending most of its time in the trees, it feeds on the inner bark of upper limbs and twigs. Telltale droppings look like wooden pellets.

5

6

7

54

8

9

10

6 *Grass Lake is a shallow lake with a marl bottom, bordered by a northern white cedar forest where spruce, balsam fir, yellow and white birch, and balm-of-Gilead (balsam poplar) are also present. Along the shoreline are large beds of sedge containing pitcher plants, false asphodel, blue flag, sweet gale, tansy, and seaside arrow grass (5-p. 53). The summer resident population of waterfowl and wading birds is sometimes increased by other flocks taking refuge from storms on nearby Lake Huron.*

7 *The purple-flowering raspberry, Rubus odoratus, might be considered the Lower Peninsula equivalent of the Upper Peninsula thimbleberry. Both plants belong to the rose family, have similar maple-shaped leaves, and bear an edible fruit. Flowers of the thimbleberry, however, are pure white.*

8 *The nest and speckled eggs of a woodcock, a small game bird, serve to emphasize the diminutive size of the dwarf lake iris.*

9 *The striped coral-root orchid, Corallorhiza striata, is one of the few plants that grow in the dense shade of the cedars.*

10 Poor conifer swamp *habitat consists of erect mature cedars so closely spaced that little sunshine reaches the ground.*

Beyond the Bridge

People say that Michigan is shaped like a mitten. This is a true statement only if one awesome natural feature is ignored—the Upper Peninsula—which many would say is the most beautiful and dramatic part of the state.

Cross the bridge and the sojourner finds himself in a world of heroic scale. He feels transported back to some Eden-like place where sky, earth, and water join forces to sustain a peaceable kingdom of man, plants, and animals living in harmony.

At the same time a traveler gains a sense of relaxation and release from everyday cares. Being far from home and with few telephones handy, he breathes the fresh air and settles down to savoring this grand "here and now."

In sheer mass the UP is equivalent to Rhode Island, Delaware, Connecticut, and Hawaii combined. Its mineral and timber resources remain enormous. In the north and west, great forests spread out from horizon to horizon.

Before Michigan became a state in 1837, the primary economic interest in the territory was the fur trade. Meanwhile copper and iron deposits had been found which started a rush of miners to the region. Lumbermen also had their eye on the vast pine forests. The UP quickly became multi-ethnic as Cornish, Finnish, Italian, French, Polish, German, Scotch, Slavic, and Scandinavian people came, giving a European flavor to the pioneer settlements.

As early as 1921 the UP was being promoted as a vacation paradise and mecca for hay fever sufferers. Tourism was greatly increased on November 1, 1957, when the former wait of hours to cross the Straits of Mackinac by ferry was changed to 10 minutes as a five-mile-long welcome mat was rolled out—the Mackinac Bridge.

Why would you want to go to so remote an area in the first place? In the UP man-made attractions are overshadowed by the glory of nature. The 37 holdings shown on the map below are fine examples of its unspoiled wild lands. A famous dolomite rock formation, the Niagaran series, forms much of the southern shoreline. Estimated to be 415 million years old, it extends south along the west shore of Lake Michigan through Wisconsin and Illinois and east through Canada to Niagara Falls. It is exposed in several places in the UP including the Garden Peninsula and Drummond Island. Many native plants which require dolomite for their habitat are protected on MNA preserves within the Niagaran Formation.

Despite its wildness, the UP is a safe place to wander. There are no poisonous snakes and few noxious plants to worry about. Depending on your interests there are countless natural wonders to see on MNA lands.

The eastern UP has its own magic. Several properties can be enjoyed with ease from road's edge—the Purple Coneflower, from M-123; the Michigan Monkey-flower, from the Epoufette Bay Road; and the open areas to the north of M-134 at Lake Huron Sand Dunes. Another easy to visit is the Twin Waterfalls Preserve. Although within the Munising city limits, it is nevertheless cut off from human bustle. Here a visitor feels himself in a natural cloister, surrounded by ancient hemlocks and accompanied by the music of the water cascades. For more strenuous excursions, you can investigate the sedge water courses of Carlton Lake where the shy loon nests, Soo Muskeg's world of sphagnum and spruce, and the windswept Lake Superior shore.

In Keweenaw, three of the most popular Class A attractions are the giant Estivant Pines, Brockway Mountain's alpine flora and hawk migrations, and the bedrock beach between Copper and Eagle Harbor.

Like its iron ore, the Upper Peninsula holds magnetic powers which, once you are under their spell, will pull you back, time and time again.

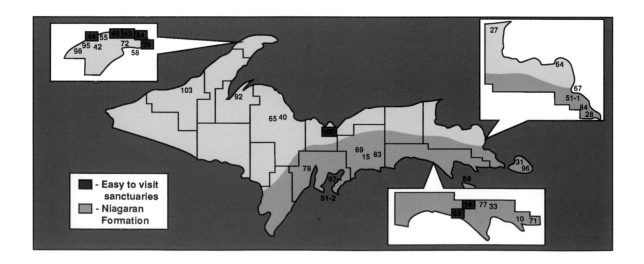

- Easy to visit sanctuaries
- Niagaran Formation

Lake Superior Nature Sanctuary

Much of the Upper Peninsula remains as wild as when Dr. Douglass Houghton explored it for copper in 1840. While his mode of travel was by canoe and foot, today we have the luxury of roads and cars. Charles W. Penny kept a journal on the Houghton trip which was later published in the book, *North to Lake Superior.* His entry for Friday, June 5th, 1840, states "...we encamped on the beach, about 12 miles from the Point..." Here he is referring to Whitefish Point, and the camp would have been in or near the present MNA holding.

Lake Superior Sanctuary contains one-half mile of **sand/ gravel beach** (above and 5, p.59), and stable dunes 11 miles west of the Point. The 369 acres in Chippewa County are a true wilderness that can be visited on an all-day trip north

from Paradise. You must have a guide for your first visit, and be prepared to walk several miles to gain access to the 500-700 foot wide beach.

The photo above, taken by Hoyt Avery shortly after the MNA purchase of 1969, shows a threesome examining the fascinating black magnetic sand which the kneeling girl is holding in her hand. This sand, made up of magnetite — iron oxide — is deposited along the coasts of the Great Lakes between layers of regular beach sand. A curiosity of this material is that it is attracted to a magnet. Several hours can be spent walking on the beach — watching the waves, finding driftwood, and looking for agates.

1   2

3

On a trip to the preserve, you walk through miles of second growth woods before reaching a 100-foot high ledge which ends at "McGregor's Cut," a sand slide leading to the beach. As you descend the path, you look down on both sides at unexplored sphagnum bogs and beaver works. Two photographers remarked about the beaver pond they explored in 1987: "We found that what appeared to be red carpeting was actually large masses of sundew growing on the shore and extending out into the water. We also discovered one-leaf rein-orchis and the leafy white orchis—two of 16 species of orchids growing here."

Next the trail leads through beds of bunchberry and up to a beach ridge. Finally, one obstacle—a 25-foot wide jungle of alders—must be crossed before you break through to the beach. The **open dunes** support many interesting plants which help stabilize the sand—beach grass, Douglas knotweed, downy goldenrod, sand cherry, pearly everlasting, beach pea, and the rare Lake Huron tansy. One plant that can be half buried in the sand and still thrive and bloom is *Hudsonia* or beach heather.

About three years ago a pair of eagles chose the Lake Superior Sanctuary for their nesting site and, in 1987, raised one eaglet. Piping plover (E) have also been successful in hatching chicks on the beach.

Jim Dorian Rooks sums up his love of this inspirational preserve in the following tribute: "I have visited the Lake Superior Sanctuary in all four seasons. Faint trails descend over broad plains of departed seas and lead to beach and dunes along Superior's shore. There are magnificent trees, wildflowers, cool hollows of land, and sunbaked blueberry plains to be savored. The smell of the north woods is all around.

"I have heard thrush, vireo, parula, blackburnian, and black-throated green warblers; seen twinflower, twayblade, arbutus, and anemone, yew and striped maple; ruffed grouse, barred owl, hooded merganser, sandhill crane; and white-tailed deer, bear and coyote. I have seen fresh workings of beaver. I have seen a bobcat and followed bobcat tracks on the beach. With all these still living in freedom here, the wilderness traveler can ask for little more."

4

5

1 *Leaves and fruit of the striped maple,* Acer pensylvanicum, *tree or shrub of the understory. It can be identified by the smooth greenish-brown bark marked with vertical white stripes.*

2 *American mountain ash,* Sorbus americana, *is a small tree of the boreal and northern hardwood forests.*

3 *One of the many valleys between beach ridges, flooded years ago by beaver, is surrounded with black spruce and tamarack.*

4 *Bracken fern and reindeer lichen form the typical ground cover of open sandy areas. The lichen is soft and spongy when damp but crunches underfoot when dry.*

5 *The Lake Superior beach is peppered with magnetic sand deposited by wave action.*

5 *The Purple Coneflower Plant Preserve in nearby Kenneth, Mackinac County, is part of an old loggers' town. The coneflower, Echinacea pallida, grows here by the side of M-123 from late summer until frost, along with leathery grapefern, pale spike lobelia, ladies'-tresses orchids, and fringed gentian, Gentiana crinita. The latter is a biennial with striking blue flowers. In June, thousands of yellow lady-slippers appear along with occasional clumps of prairie cinquefoil, turning the preserve into a tapestry of gold.*

Eastern Upper Peninsula Specialties

1 *Michigan monkey-flower, Mimulus glabratus var. michiganensis (T, T-USA), is one of the rarest plants in the world, found in only one environment—in pure streams coming out of cedar swamps in a few counties near the Straits of Mackinac. The MNA preserve for it is near Epoufette. It is a tall showy variety of the more common little yellow monkey-flower, with a long bloom period extending into early October.*

2 *MNA has two preserves with Hill's thistle, Cirsium hillii (SC). In its original habitat,* **sand prairie,** *it has practically disappeared from its original range in the midwest. In the Upper Peninsula of Michigan it has spread from farms on Drummond Island to rocky woods openings. Such a site is the MNA Harvey's Rocks Preserve, where several hundred of these beauties can be found. It is a native thistle not shown in most plant books; it blooms on stems from 5 to 12 inches tall.*

3 *The Lapland Buttercup Plant Preserve in Chippewa County is one of only two known Michigan locations for Ranunculus lapponicus (T), an arctic-alpine species normally found from Canada north to Greenland. Inconspicuous and only two to four inches tall, it grows at the edge of small pools of water in a cedar swamp but where there is no sphagnum moss. Because it blooms at the same time as goldthread, it is sometimes difficult to tell which is which. The flower of the lapland buttercup, however, is distinctly golden—that of the goldthread, white (although its root is golden). The buttercup has prettily scalloped leaves.*

4 *Sandhill cranes congregate at an MNA project near Rudyard, Chippewa County, to rest on their fall migration route to southwest U.S. and Mexico. One of Michigan's largest birds, sandhills stand over three feet tall with a wing-spread of 6 to 7 feet. The young are overall brown in color; adults are slate gray with a red "cap." While feeding they make a low loud musical rattle which can be heard from afar.*

Rare Fern Plant Preserve

Gaining title to this land of rock and fern in Mackinac County climaxed a 15-year effort by the MNA to fend off vacation home development in the area. Geologically it is part of the Niagaran Escarpment (see page 56) whose sedimentary rocks contain a large proportion of dolomite, a mineral composed of calcium and magnesium carbonates. Characteristically, an above-ground formation runs in a series of low ledges (1) accompanied by free-standing boulders from 6 to 16 feet high. This habitat is called a **boulder field.** These rocks are the locale for the American hart's-tongue fern, *Phyllitis scolopendrium* var. *americana* (E, E-USA) (3). Structurally the hart's-tongue differs from other fern species. Its thick evergreen leaf blades are simple. Other plants in close association with the hart's-tongue are the holly fern, walking fern, and herb-Robert geranium.

Exploring the preserve can be a scary adventure, because it is part of a vast wilderness where a seasoned woodsman can get lost. In broad daylight, if your traveling companion moves out of sight, contact can be broken very easily since the terrain is monotonous and without significant landmarks, and voices have a ventriloquist effect. Bear, snowy owls, and ravens have been encountered. This is no preserve for the novice naturalist and is designated "C" category in the MNA classification system.

The green spleenwort fern, *Asplenium viride* (SC), (2), grows at the preserve on its low moss-covered limestone outcroppings in a maple forest where there is little ground cover. The plant is hard to find both because of its small size (note the size compared to violet leaf) and its great scarcity. It is easily confused with maidenhair spleenwort but the green spleenwort has green axes and upper stalks.

1

2

3

1

2

Lake Huron Sand Dunes
Plant Preserve

This engaging preserve is located between Cedarville and Detour on M-134 east of M-48 in Chippewa County. There are numerous public sites along the road affording scenic views of Lake Huron. The MNA ownership consists of frontage on the north side of the highway and 15.6 acres of sand dunes. Park your car on the lake side at the turn-around. Observe the thicket of stunted, windswept balsam poplars, *Populus balsamifera*, (also called tacahamac, balm-of-Gilead, or just plain "bam") anchoring the dune. The close-up picture (1) shows the bam's weathered leaves in autumn. The terminal, rust-colored, winter buds are often one inch long and covered with a resinous substance that wafts a sweet fragrance in the air. The tree is ubiquitous in the north in disturbed soils, especially along roadsides.

2 *The ram's head orchid,* Cypripedium arietinum *(SC), grows in protected areas of ground cover such as pipsissewa, trailing arbutus, and pyrola. It blooms around Memorial Day. The calypso orchid, blooming about a week earlier, grows in the same area.*

3 *On the sheltered side of the second and third dunes from the lake, beds of bunchberry,* Cornus canadensis, *cover the sand beneath the towering pines. The waxy white flower heads and bright green fleshy leaves are clear signs of the plant's membership in the dogwood family. The scarlet fruits appear in late summer.*

3

This preserve has **open dunes** habitat (6) where dunes, once moving, are being stabilized by scattered clumps of beach grass and, slightly farther inland, with sand cherry, zygadenus, Pitcher's thistle, and starry solomon's seal.

The second dune from the lakeshore is a high ridge of what could be called Great Lakes barrens, with white and red pine, white spruce and balsam fir, and ground cover of common and horizontal juniper and reindeer lichen (4). Between this and the third dune, false heather, *Hudsonia tomentosa*, and spiral ladies' tresses orchids grow, and a lucky person might find pinedrops, *Pterospora* (5), which blooms sporadically in August.

At the back and west of the third dune is a small, swift stream, lined with white cedars and spanned by fallen logs, which has cut a ravine bordered by spurred gentian, northern commandra, heart-leaved twayblade orchids, clintonia, cow-wheat, and pink pyrola.

This is a B-C type preserve that should be visited first with a guide. However, once the landmarks are located it is always possible to make a brief stop in passing. The lure to spend a few moments in these glorious surroundings is irresistible. Such a visitor, however, should restrict himself to areas within sight of the lake as the terrain farther inland, though not difficult to maneuver, is a good place to get "turned around." In the back 16 acres contact with civilization is lost and a delightful sense of isolation pervades. Five crests of old beach lines—ridges showing the successive stages of the lake edge as the glaciers retreated—go back a quarter-mile to an overlook of a vast watery expanse of cedar and tamarack swamps.

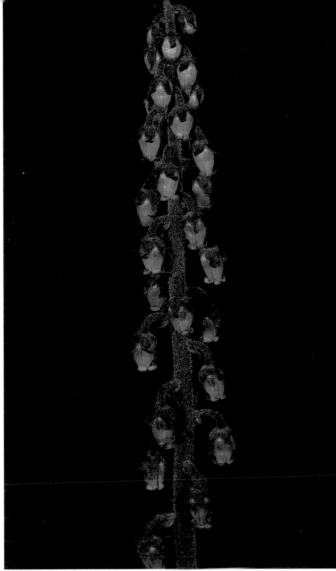

4

5

6

1 2

3

4

5

Harvey's Rocks Plant Preserve
(also called Cobble Beach)

Harvey Ballard, Jr. found this stretch of rock beach for the MNA in 1985. It is a perfect example of a subtype of bedrock beach, **cobble beach** habitat (1) that occurs along portions of shoreline around Drummond Island and the south coast of the eastern Upper Peninsula. In this situation, a bizarre assemblage of calcium-loving plants grows—fen, marsh, interdunal swale, dune, and boreal type species. Along with other more common flora are lush growths of the sedge *Carex scirpoidea* (T), which varies in height from 4 to 18 inches, and the prairie dropseed grass, *Sporobolus heterolepis* (T). Ohio goldenrod, *Solidago ohioensis* (2), can be seen growing in (1), left center.

This preserve has a large expanse of horizontal alvar pavement and limestone cobble beach dotted with small stranded pools of water (4). It is a jewel of a place, so absorbing for the plant lover walking with bated breath and wondering where to step next. Vista after vista unfolds, each more beguiling than the last.

Frequent fogs add to the mystery. Sunsets are sometimes spectacular. Rocks, both large and small, bear brilliant orange lichens (5). Other rocks have small round lichens that gleam like polished silver.

If you go inland from the beach, you pass through a tranquil glade of white cedar (3), silent but for the occasional flutelike song of the hermit thrush. On its border grows the Richardson's sedge, *Carex richardsonii* (SC). A colony of Hill's thistle (T) is a bonus (see page 60).

1

2   3

Carlton Lake Wetlands Nature Sanctuary

This property of 400 acres (page 66) is southeast of Goetzville in Chippewa County. Known to few and hidden far from civilization, its unobstructed vistas of northern forest borders and teeming wildlife delight and challenge canoeists and birdwatchers.

Carlton Lake is actually a very large beaver pond, shallow and reedy, that did not exist before the late 20's. Over 45 species of resident birds include American and least bittern, ring-necked duck, black tern, green-backed heron, winter and sedge wren, pied-billed grebe, and sandhill crane. Bobolinks are plentiful in the shorter sedges. It is the one MNA preserve recommended for overnight camping—to permit leisurely bird study.

Edna Newnan recalls, "In order to explore this huge water wilderness our group portaged over a quarter mile of logging trail to the tributary river north of the lake, then paddled a mile south to the preserve entrance. Because of the sequestered nature of the area, it is ideal habitat for such shy water birds as Virginia and sora rails. Moving silently across the lake, we thrilled to hear the banshee cries of a pair of nesting loons; from the sedge and sweet gale flats a deer started for cover in the northern forest that borders the east side of the preserve."

1 *Two hikers pick their way through mucky sedge flats toward the higher land in the foreground where a tamarack branch can be seen.*

2 *Sheep laurel,* Kalmia angustifolia, *grows in large patches. A member of the heath family, it resembles a rhododendron. Sometimes called "lambkill," because it is toxic to animals.*

3 *Fawn nestled in tall grasses.*

Soo Muskeg Nature Sanctuary

This preserve of 80 acres in Chippewa County is four miles southwest of Sault Ste. Marie. The word "muskeg" is an Ojibway Indian name for a kind of bog or marsh formed by the deposit of thick layers of decaying matter in a depression. **Muskeg** is a subtype of open bog habitat.

In (2) below, visitors walk on the mossy hummocks in between pools of standing water. Exploring the colorful area is fun, but rubber boots are recommended, and a compass is a must. It is not a good place to walk alone or get separated from companions. (1) shows a stand of black spruce; in other sections there are tamarack and white pine.

The terrain is variable. The southern third is wet, with alders and acres of marsh marigolds in spring; the other two-thirds is higher ground and bog. Pink moccasin flowers are plentiful.

Star of the preserve is the *Aster nemoralis* (T) (3). Discovered here on an MNA field trip in 1981, it has a vivid pink flower with irregular petals. Its blooming peak is about September 4. Only one muskeg opening has been found containing the plant. *Selaginella selaginoides,* an arctic-alpine species, also grows here.

1

2

3

1   2

3

Bertha K. Daubendiek Memorial Plant Preserve

Because beaver works shut off access, this 360 feet of frontage on the Escanaba River, Delta County, can be reached only by wading the 400-foot wide river or approaching by canoe from the downriver Cornell fishing site.

The rock-ribbed and rock-bottomed Escanaba is carved by water action through the Niagaran formation. Despite water level now being controlled by dams, the river retains much of its original untamed grandeur. To watch a great blue heron fish in its shallows, see gulls stand quietly on lonely rocks out in the rushing water, or hear a kingfisher rattle across its mighty expanse is a thrill.

This is an **open alvar** habitat site (3). Alvar is produced by scouring of the bedrock by glaciers. The almost flat plates of limestone bedrock extend back from the river pavements but are exposed here. A 40-foot wide border of slippery, striated limestone with strange and wonderful flora extends from the water to 25-foot high cliff banks. Wet meadow and limestone-loving species grow here, and at the water's edge are the wild chives, *Alium schoenoprasum* (T) (6), an arctic plant.

Bertha A. Daubendiek reminisces: *"It scarcely seems possible that such a tiny piece of land—only .3 of an acre—could give so much pleasure and enlightenment as this one does. This MNA Project No. 78 was the one I was working on at the time my mother, Bertha Krejci Daubendiek, died. She lived in Iowa but on annual vacations to Michigan had walked everywhere I did on our preserves since the beginning. Our family arranged for this place to become a memorial for her. She was a member and one of MNA's first and best boosters."*

"When we came to dedicate the sanctuary on May 27, 1985, it was cold, wet, and windy. We waited five days at Rapid River until the weather cleared and was just right to get up by canoe from the Cornell access. It was warm along the south-facing shore; wild columbine was in bloom and hummingbirds were darting about."

"Mom would have liked this spot for she was a fisherwoman who loved wild places. The buffaloberries by the Escanaba River would remind her of our Montana homestead region. All my life I heard her talk about gathering them out on the coulees to make jelly. She would have been thrilled by the rocks, the climb above to the jack pines, and seeing the view from the high part along the river."

"I find it vastly invigorating to go to this preserve. I enjoy seeing the phoebe at its natural nest ledge on a vertical cliff face, where masses of bladder ferns grow. Never once have I gone there that an osprey has not appeared, soaring overhead seemingly curious about the human activity below. It is an intriguing place—full of delightful surprises."

4

6

5

There is a high quality prairie area along the shore of Indian grass, prairie cord-grass, little and big bluestem, and Richardson's muhly-grass (T). Most unusual are clumps of Sporobolus heterolepis *(T) (see reddish tops in 3 and 4). (2) shows its flower and (1) its seed. On the seed head look for the hard, roundish balls which are the plant's distinguishing characteristic.*

Myrtle Justeson Memorial Nature Sanctuary
(formerly Willow Creek)

In the rugged country north of Marquette this "long 40," meaning a piece of land one-eighth mile wide and one-half mile long, has a great enough sampling of rock, swamp, and stream to make up an absorbing all day trip. Getting here by way of County 510 and Deer Lake Roads, is half the fun, and exploring time goes fast. To begin with, you never know whether all the culverts are intact to take you there; if some have washed out you will have to walk an extra mile to get in. This is no hardship, as the way is on old logging trails. After reaching the property, the sandy soil has no obstacles, and there is much to see: trailing arbutus, ground pines, pink moccasin flowers, and lowbush blueberries. Woodcock are plentiful and may surprise you by taking off with a rasping noise as you pass through. The object is to reach the **rock escarpment** (3) and enjoy the superb views. The cliff is north of the creek and up to 80 feet high, part of a three-mile-long promontory in country not too far from Ropes Gold Mine. (The rocks have been analyzed and found to contain small traces of gold.) One of the nicest points about the sanctuary is that it is dead end. Once you have reached your destination all traffic has long since ceased behind you. The escarpment finally comes too close to Willow Creek to permit a road, so the last part is merely a narrow foot trail.

1

2

3   4

5

Bertha Daubendiek remarks, "There are many reasons and many seasons to visit this sanctuary north of Marquette, but one highly recommended is the peak of the fall color which begins here October 1.

"On October 5, 1986, Sue Bolm of Marquette and I met Tom Buchkoe of Big Bay for the purpose of coming back with a picture of the **rock escarpment** habitat. While Tom and Sue disappeared on that quest, I experimented with capturing the scene spread out before me along the edges of Willow Creek; (2) is the result.

"The water flows cold and pure, but its level varies greatly from year to year. I had previously taken a scene from the very same spot (4) in August of 1979. On that day, the water was so low we could walk right into the middle of the stream. On the edges of the creek, lobelia, goldenrod, aster, and Joe-Pye-weed made a riot of color.

"(3) shows the rock wall that Tom photographed. While Tom was taking his picture, I had wandered up near him and caught largetooth aspens (1) in the late afternoon sun. (Note in photo 2 that far in the distance a bluish-mauve haze has settled over the hills, where the maples have already shed their leaves.)

"(5) was taken in the fall of 1987 from a spot 200 feet higher and looking down over the tops of spires of pines and spruce below.

"To reach this overlook is not as hard as you might think. You go beyond where both (3) and (4) were taken, some hundreds of feet to where a side stream comes down a valley once used to float logs to Willow Creek. Look up the valley for a dead cedar tree, go back west toward the escarpment, and start climbing up slant-wise along the fairly easy slope, which is a place where water pours down after rains. When you reach the highest point, move forward to the front of the ledge and enjoy the view."

1

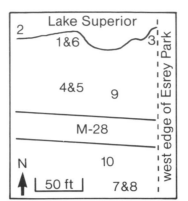

This map of a one acre area of Keweenaw Shore No. 1 Nature Sanctuary shows the locations where photos 1 through 10 were taken.

1 *Charles Eshbach, renowned Upper Peninsula photographer from Houghton, prepares to take a seascape of Lake Superior. Staunch supporter of the MNA, he and Ralph Polovich of Port Huron have been given honorary membership status in recognition of their many years of outstanding camera work for the organization. Charlie is standing on top of the very same rock shown on the left side of (6). (3) was taken on the opposite side of the cove.*

Keweenaw Shore No. 1 Nature Sanctuary

Florence Lewis, summer resident for 44 years in the Eagle Harbor environs, describes her perceptions of this area: "The Keweenaw Peninsula thrusts a rocky finger into the cold waters of Lake Superior midway along its southern shore. Down the middle of the peninsula the Copper Range of mountains seems to have been squeezed into being by the icy lake on either side. Shorelines are mainly a fascinating jumble of volcanic and sedimentary rocks that are the oldest exposed anywhere in Michigan. Through eons of time they have been hammered by crashing waves and split apart by freezing ice. Nevertheless, irrepressible wildflowers, shrubs, and grasses, though stunted by wind and wave, flourish wherever a sediment of earth fills a rock fissure. The craggy mountainsides are heavily forested."

With the encouraging help of Keweenaw friends, the MNA was able to establish nine projects here in the same number of years, from 1973 to 1982. Some are outstanding enough to have been nominated for distinction as National Natural Landmarks.

Three MNA properties, Keweenaw Shore Nos. 1 and 2, and Hylton Memorial, are located on the north side of the Peninsula in the five-mile stretch between Eagle and Copper Harbor. All feature **bedrock beach** habitat (2) where the dramatic wave-battered layers of ancient lava interbedded with conglomerate rock dominate the shoreline, sloping sharply out of the lake in partially submerged ridges. These ghosts of primeval tumult create the southern rim of the great syncline that forms the bed of Lake Superior between Isle Royale and the Keweenaw.

Keweenaw Shore No. 1, on the west edge of Esrey Park, a well-known scenic vantage point on the coast, safeguards a 475-foot stretch of shoreline surmounted by a rampart of timeless coastal rock, perpetually besieged by the lake's breakers. The cove at the sanctuary is prized by photographers for its unobstructed views of Superior's glorious sunrises and sunsets (3). Inland from M-26 the MNA property extends southward on a broadened front over ever-mounting ridges, embracing 37 acres of unspoiled woodland. After reaching the highest point of land, it descends steeply to Brockway Mountain Drive opposite Upson Lake Sanctuary.

2

2 *On the **bedrock beach** exposure to storms keeps the outer rocks clean of everything except, as here, the most tenacious roots of juniper shrubs (foreground).*

3

4

5

4 & 5 *The black haw,* Crataegus douglasii *(SC), is a small tree or shrub bearing clusters of white flowers in May, followed by glossy black fruit. Regularly growing in the Rocky Mountains and found only sparsely in the Lake Superior region, it is classed as a disjunct species in this locale.*

6 *In April the Keweenaw's basalt coast is still frozen into a titanic ice sculpture.*

7 & 8 *Usnea lichen can be observed in only a few locations in the Keweenaw. Moisture-laden winds from the lake produce the cool, humid atmospheric conditions where it can grow. Just a few feet into the woods at Keweenaw Shore No. 1, directly across the road from where pictures (1-6 and 9) were taken, you can see strands of it draped over conifers, creating an eerie effect. The light green* usnea *covers tree bark and branches with a dense beard-like growth often over a foot long.*

7

6

8

9

10

9 *Thimbleberry,* Rubus parviflorus, *is an Upper Penin-sula specialty. On a summer hike the juicy red berries make for an on-the-spot delicious trail-food or you can take them home for pie filling and next winter's jam.*

10 *A balsam fir seedling shoots up from a moist crevice between the lichen-covered rocks.*

11 **Northern boreal forest** *habitat occurs on a half dozen MNA properties, one in the northern Lower Peninsula and five in the Upper Peninsula. The most*

important trees found in this habitat are balsam fir, white spruce, white birch, white pine and white cedar. Ground-layer species are abundant and include red baneberry, bead-lily, trailing clubmoss, stiff clubmoss, sweet colt's-foot, and one-flowered wintergreen. This photo was taken on the high rocky back of Keweenaw Shore No. 1 where it overlooks Brockway Mountain Drive. It is across the road from the **dry northern forest** *habitat picture shown on page 89.*

11

1

2

Eagle Harbor Red Pines Dunes Nature Sanctuary

One of the latest MNA acquisitions in the Keweenaw, this preserve is underlain by dunes. Here pink moccasin flowers grow in a cushiony carpet of juniper and club mosses beneath the evergreens. Five acres contain a pure stand of lovely red pine with a view of Lake Superior from its highest point. Ladies from Eagle Harbor enjoy strolling on the carefree hiking trail to the main dune ridge and to the bog (1). In winter the area provides good skiing.

2 *Needles of red pine, 4 to 6 inches long, occur in pairs and remain on the branch for up to five years.*
3 *Sharp tips distinguish leaves of the red oak—the only oak growing in the Keweenaw. Emerging red and velvety in the spring, they turn from lustrous summer green to vivid russet again in autumn.*

Upson Lake Nature Sanctuary

Beaver, coyote, and other wildlife roam this 100-acre wilderness tract. Unmarred by signs of human habitation, views from the north shore include steep wooded hillsides across the lake and to "Brockway's Nose", a rocky prominence on the horizon to the east. White birches are plentiful (4) along the creek.

3

4

1 *The bird's-eye primrose,* Primula mistassinica *Michx., blooms in early June along the rock shore of Lake Superior in Keweenaw. Standing 6 to 10 inches tall in crevices of the inner rocks, this small wildflower is pink with a yellow central "eye" and five notched petals. The tiny winter rosette which can be seen throughout the year is a clear identification mark. It is a pleasure to find the gay pink bird's-eye in early spring and marvel at its ability to survive the recent rigors of winter's ice and cold on the barren rock. The species can also be found on MNA preserves at Drummond Island, Beavertail Point, and Grass Lake, where the primrose comes into full flower as early as the week before Memorial Day.*

1

2

2 *"It was just a chance friendly encounter, August 8th of 1987. I made a quick stop, your parents' van came along and I asked you to pose. That is the rare mountain alder, or green alder,* Alnus crispa, *you are looking at, growing on the inner edge of where small "bam" trees, balsam poplar, line M 26. Thank you, Wisconsin vacationers, I didn't even ask your name. Thank you, two merry sisters— fashion-conscious teen-ager and little sister with the impish grin. It was an enjoyable moment we shared."—B.A.D.*

3 *The developing seed heads of the nine-bark are sharp-tipped and deep pink in color. This native shrub, often cultivated in the home garden, comes as a surprise when you find it growing on this rugged, northernmost shore. A member of the rose family with a widespread distribution throughout the state, it thrives in such varied locations as the lush streambanks of Helmer Brook Prairie near Kalamazoo, and Shannon Nature Sanctuary, where it reaches 10 feet in height. It is so hardy that it can survive temperatures of −50 degrees Fahrenheit in the Canadian provinces. Nine-bark commands attention when in bloom with its white, spirea-like flowers borne in almost spherical clusters, and later, when the seed heads are full.*

3

Keweenaw Shore No. 2 at Dan's Point

This project shares the same **bedrock beach** formation with nearby Hylton Memorial and Keweenaw Shore No. 1, four miles to the west. Hylton and Dan's Point each have 165 feet of shoreline on Lake Superior but extend 2100 feet inland across M-26.

Dan's Point is the most northern point on the mainland of Michigan. The rocks that go down into Lake Superior at a 30 degree angle (4) dip under the lake water and come out 35 miles away on Isle Royale, — at the opposite 30 degree angle. This geological feature, known as the "angle of Keweenaw," is boldly displayed here.

(4) was taken June 21, 1980, the day the preserve was dedicated, along with five other close-by MNA projects. All can be reached in a half day by car (see map page 93). In foreground, wearing blue jeans and carrying a walking stick, is Dave Oullette, registrar of Houghton's Michigan Tech University, who first told MNA about this spot. He typifies some 50 or more persons who have given worthwhile "tips" to the MNA. Most of the shrubs growing on the rock are nine-bark and sweet gale, dwarfed by their constant fight against the elements.

To drive here, look for a pink cottage with blue mailbox on the inland side of M-26. The preserve is almost opposite. Park at the tiny lakeside pull-off, and slip through the border of "bam" trees edged with seven-foot green alders. The bams are shrub-size "whips" giving off the sweet pungent smell of their sticky buds. This is one of the choicest small MNA preserves, a true delight for whatever time or season visited.

Ahead of you, a barely visible path leads onto the purplish colored rocks where the going is rough. To your astonishment you find the many cracks and crevices are filled with plants. There are grasses, sedges, and rushes, all difficult to identify. But among the surprising little things that grow in the rocks, along with lichens galore, are unusual flowers easy to find: sand violet, *Viola adunca,* three-toothed cinquefoil, *Potentilla tridentata,* and the goldenrod, *Solidago spathulata ssp. randii,* here a mere two inches high on the exposed rocks. In two special protected bands grow butterworts, *Pinguicula vulgaris* (SC). Bright yellow-green, the leaves near the base remind one of the color of butter.

Dan's Point is a study in contrasts—it is small and intimate—yet on the edge of the crashing Lake Superior surf. If you have a sense of daring you can climb onto the highest rock at Dan's Point—then quickly get back into your car. This is the place where year-round residents seek out the cold rocky shore at the time of winter storms. When giant waves lash the outer rocks, wind-washed sheets of spray can be watched from the safety of an automobile.

The inland part of the preserve lies across M-26 and goes way back. Take compass and topo map. There is enough to occupy a whole day, going up over successive ridges to the base of Brockway Mountain. Enjoy every minute of it. If you have started up going south by compass take a compass reading west for the eighth of a mile that separates the two preserves. Then come back down again on the Hylton side. Be aware that bears travel the unused military road you will cross.

4

1

3

Brockway Mountain Nature Sanctuary

From Copper Harbor, drive southeast on scenic highway US-41 to the crossing of Garden Brook (1), a small stream which flows through the preserve (see map, p. 93). In late summer it is refreshing to stand on its hemlock-edged bank and listen to the murmur of the flowing water.

Brockway Mountain Sanctuary was established to protect some important plant species found in Michigan only in Keweenaw County. The Whitney's or heart-leaved arnica, *Arnica cordifolia (Arnica whitneyi)* (T) (2), is a perennial with canary yellow, daisy-like flowers about two inches across which, after blooming, develop fluffy seed heads like those of dandelions. Another unusual plant here is deerbush or wild-lilac, *Ceanothus sanguineus* (T) (3), a flowering shrub of the buckthorn family not to be confused with domestic lilac. It is classed as an isolated relic-species because it is separated by hundreds of miles from the nearest station in the Black Hills of South Dakota.

The view from the Sanctuary shown in (4) looks east toward Lake Fanny Hooe from a vantage point atop the cliff just south of Brockway Mountain Drive. The mountain is the highest point of the ages-old Copper Range, older than the Appalachians and worn down by time. The rocky, rugged slopes are forested with stands of pine, birch, maple, oak, and poplar, plus a scattering of other tree species.

4

1

2

3

James H. Klipfel Memorial Nature Sanctuary

This preserve lies only a few hundred yards from the west summit of Brockway Mountain. From the popular vantage point of the Klipfel pull-off can be seen one of the most dramatic panoramas in the midwest. Contained within 160 acres open to the sky at Klipfel is a half-mile segment of towering rock face, a habitat classified as **sandstone conglomerate subtype** of rock formation (3).

At Klipfel almost any day of the year when you step out of your car you face cold, sharp wind. The vegetation here is stunted by the grueling winds and an inhospitable environment of all rock, best suited for arctic and alpine species—grasses, sedges, ground covers and dwarfed shrubs— that can survive under the most trying conditions.

The purple cliff-brake fern, *Pellaea atropurpurea* (T) (2), occurs in only a few places in the Upper Peninsula. It was discovered by Charles Eshbach in 1978, growing at the Klipfel Memorial on an almost perpendicular wall of rock far below the top of the cliff. Here the fern has found a niche it likes, a very dry, sunny place on exposed conglomerate rock. Under the drought-like conditions only single plants grow, scattered here and there. Few people will ever see this fern because, as one tenderfoot expressed it, "You have to risk your life to go there."

On Klipfel is another type of rock habitat, known as **bald**. Consisting of rotted rock, nothing will grow on it except a tiny flower, the small blue-eyed Mary, *Collinsia parviflora* (T) (1). At the end of May, the equivalent of earliest spring in southwestern Michigan where the blue-eyed Mary, *Collinsia verna*, is first starting to bloom (page 30), the flowers of the miniscule *C. parviflora* appear. So tiny, they are the size of ants. Charlotte Catoni of Eagle Harbor, who took the photo, all bundled up against gusty winds, invites other close-up photographers to come up and "do better."

Other plant specialties at Klipfel are Houghton's and Richardson's sedge (SC), little grape fern, moonwort fern, and green adder's mouth orchid.

From the end of March until mid-June, a spectator at the Klipfel overlook has a ringside seat to watch migrating birds of prey return from wintering areas in the south to their breeding grounds in Canada.

In the Keweenaw, the south-facing cliffs of Brockway Mountain are heated by the sun, creating updrafts that are sought out and exploited by the soaring hawks; the birds can be seen mounting the thermal currents to great heights.

81

Estivant Pines Nature Sanctuary

The Keweenaw is known throughout the world as the fabled "Copper Country" where from prehistoric times through the first part of the Twentieth Century, Indians and later, miners sought its pure red-gold ore. Three miles south of Copper Harbor are the Estivant Pines—a classic stand of huge virgin white pines. The forest is named for a Frenchman, Edouard Estivant, who purchased 2400 acres of heavy timber in the region in the 1870's. The land remained in his family until 1947 when it was acquired by the Calumet & Hecla Mining Company, which merged in 1968 with Universal Oil Products. A subsidiary, Goodman Lumber Company, started cutting the remaining Estivant Pines in 1970.

The Michigan Nature Association, which was then just getting acquainted with the area, learned of the local protest and joined with a Keweenaw committee to save the pines. Under the leadership of Bertha Daubendiek, Richard Holzman, Charlie Eshbach and Jim Rooks, a successful three-year campaign was waged to wrest this "forest primeval" from corporate interests.

Now, six thousand people—all ages and from all parts of Michigan, many of them repeat visitors—walk through this sanctuary annually. Kewecnaw residents have voted it their favorite attraction, ranking it over the nearby Isle Royale National Park.

EPITAPH

A Tribute To The Leaning Giant
by Kernie King

"On October 8, 1987, I was told the Leaning Giant had fallen to the ground, due to a fierce 24-hour north wind. This news brought back memories of the first and only time I visited that magnificent white pine tree, on May 26, 1985.

I made several photographs from its best side, as the other side of the trunk was severely charred from a fire October, 1980 (3), started by a careless hiker. Also, a long crack had developed along the trunk. I placed my hand over the crack and felt some movement, as if the tree had a heartbeat. Actually the movement was from a breeze in the tree tops more than 100 feet overhead. At that time I wondered how much longer this tree could survive. Now that it has fallen, maybe one of its seeds will grow to become a giant 400 or 500 years from now for someone else to enjoy as I did."

Crowning jewel of the Estivants was the "Leaning Giant" (pictured at left and 3, opposite page). This monarch of trees measured almost eight feet in diameter, stood 120 feet tall, and was estimated to be over 500 years old. It was verified as Michigan's champion white pine in August, 1971. Its Pisa-like stance and great size have been attributed to its position on the bank of the Montreal River: the rich bottomland provided extra nutrients for the tree but fed its root system unevenly, thus producing lopsided growth.

1

1 *Hiking in this 200-acre remnant, you discover a living museum of ancient trees as you tread the pristine forest trail. At the gateway to the "Cathedral Grove" in the heart of the sanctuary, the straight ghostly trunks of the huge pines appear on every side. There are over 900 of these "elder statesmen" in the thick backdrop of sugar maple and yellow* birch. *Only one percent can be seen from any given vantage point, since they are scattered in 22 groves of from 20 to 90 individual trees.*

2 *Thimbleberry, Rubus parviflorus, grows in the northern Great Lakes region and then does not reappear until the Black Hills and Rocky Mountains.*

2   3

1 *Photographer Gary Giannunzio writes, "An awkward bird flew clumsily past, landing on a fir. Gangling fowl, the blue heron has great powers of flight on longer journeys. Wary creature with acute hearing and telescopic sight, posing statue like, it feeds in quiet, ancient places, solitary. The primal, classic sage is a whisper of long time past."*

2 *Hikers at the summit of Bear Bluff enjoy the forest in fall colors and the view across Bete Gris Bay of Point Isabelle to the southwest.*

Russell and Miriam Grinnell Memorial Nature Sanctuary

Within the boundaries of this preserve lies most of the summit of Bare Bluff, a giant monolith that rises nearly 600 feet above Lake Superior. Shown on early maps as Bare Hill, it is the most prominent landmark along the south shore of the Keweenaw Peninsula.

From a vantage point high on the bluff the onlooker enjoys 180 degree panorama of Lake Superior. The magnificent view toward Keweenaw Point appears on the jacket of this book.

Toward the lake, the massive felsite face of Bare Bluff rises dramatically from a forested coastal terrace in a sheer vertical precipice over 200 feet high. From the brow of the cliff, barren outcrops scoured by ancient glaciers slope sharply up and away toward the wooded summit. The lichen-encrusted rocks exposed to rigors of the Keweenaw climate offer scant living to a few hardy plants and low shrubs, whose roots cling tenaciously in cracks and crannies.

Marked differences in elevation within the sanctuary, and its proximity to the crashing surf of Lake Superior, have produced a variety of unusual habitats, each with its unique flora. Rare and interesting plants survive on the exposed **bald** habitat near the summit and in the niches of the bluff. Worth noting are small blue-eyed Mary, trail plant (a Keweenaw disjunct), the grass *Trisetum spicatum*, the male fern, and the expanded wood fern.

For the nature lover who relishes spectacular scenery and a challenging itinerary, the way to the summit of Bear Bluff via primitive road and rugged trail is indeed a highway to fulfillment.

Kenneth W. and Timothy S. Gunn Memorial Nature Sanctuary

This property also presents a broad vista of the awesome remote stretch of Lake Superior shoreline from Bare Bluff to Keweenaw Point (3). Look at a Michigan map and study the lay of the land in which these epic MNA preserves are situated. First find Keweenaw Point on the tip of the southeast shore. Going west five miles is the site of the Gunn property from whose coast picture (3) was taken. Looking at the photo, find Bare Bluff, the high knob with whitish cliff faces in the distant upper left.

The preserves can be reached in different ways. It is easy to get a splendid distant view of Bare Bluff and Fish Lake Cove by boat from the lake. It is recommended that you attempt to explore the Gunn/Grinnell wilderness only with a guide, as it is classified in the MNA's "most challenging" category.

At Gunn Memorial the prime attraction is a massive outcropping of reddish volcanic rock (felsite or rhyolite) on the east side of Fish Cove. State Biologist L. L. Hubbard visited it in 1898, mapped it, and named it Fish Cove Knob.

From its base along the shore of Lake Superior, the Knob, covering an area of roughly 16 acres, rises to an elevation of about 90 feet. It is covered with wildflowers, mosses, and lichens, and backed by white pines, spruces, and other trees in the higher reaches. A small wave-sculpted stack called Indian Head is a picturesque feature of the shoreline.

Another dramatic characteristic of the Gunn sanctuary is pictured in the foreground rocks which appear to be standing almost on end. These typify a geological structure called columnar jointing, which may occur when cracks are generated during rapid and uniform cooling of lava injected into a fissure. The cracks tend to divide the solidifying magma into long, hexagonal columns perpendicular to the walls of the fault.

Such are the facts about Grinnell and Gunn, but they do little to convey the aura of expansiveness and unfettered natural beauty that so charm a visitor.

The following lyrical account was written by Gary Giannunzio of Norway, Michigan, describing his feelings as he drank in the wonders of the Grinnell and Gunn environs:

"A place of mesmerizing mystery and mad magic is the Keweenaw Peninsula's Superior shore…The images haunt my mind. Bare Bluff…facing the morning sun, glows brilliant, warm, and golden above the shadowed shoreline. Fresh and fine dawn. The morning mist on wild daisy petals, moist red ripe raspberries and thimbleberries, meadow grass-blades glisten, cloud wisps fading into blue sky, sun sitting passive and primitive, vital morning, unpeopled land. The shore trail was strewn wild with branched white cedar in all growth stages, from birth to decay. Multicolored lichens and lush mosses carpet protrusions of rhyolite."

The icy chill of the lake water is an invigorating gateway to fine stone, sand, bouldered, bedrock beaches. Past the harebells with their spilling-out cups, past sugar plum shores to Indian Rock…and beyond, feeling at times akin to Robinson Crusoe, the broad sweep of a pebbled beach seemed part of a lost world. Forgotten havens, little changed since time's earliest dawns, peacefulness, gem-colored stones magnified by crystal water, heart's-mind images of the original people make a dreamland. Washing water upon the shore, smooth agate touch, soul-stirring. Touch this land quickly and gently and she will call you to return."

The Scientific Significance of the Michigan Nature Association Program

An evaluation by Harvey Ballard, Jr., Professional Botanist

"To this date the Michigan Nature Association (MNA) is the only wholly in-state citizen group (i.e., without national affiliation) which owns and maintains a system of nature preserves.*** [It] established its first preserve, Red Wing Acres, in 1960 and has since accumulated over 55 preserves (more than any other single organization in Michigan)."

This statement by Susan R. Crispin, on p. 109 of her 1980 review of Michigan's most significant protected natural areas, *(Michigan Botanist* Vol. 19, pp 99-242), summarizes the MNA's outstanding achievements to that time.

Crispin's study was the first ever made of all nature preserves established in the state since 1920. Of 156 natural areas preserved up through 1979, Crispin found 20 owned by various U.S. government agencies, 32 by the State of Michigan agencies, seven by local governments, 18 by The Nature Conservancy, seven by Michigan Audubon Society, and nine by colleges and universities. *A surprising 57 areas were owned by the MNA.*

Since 1980 MNA has added more sanctuaries, bringing its current total to 107 in over half of Michigan's 83 counties. Totals for the various other entities in Crispin's study (including a few new local conservancies established in the eight year interim) have not increased to any degree. The MNA's approach to selection of natural areas, a program carried out almost exclusively by knowledgeable volunteers, has been simple and effective. It can serve as a model for any group to follow.

When the selection of the initial five sanctuaries was made in 1960, and up through the first 25 projects, the only guideline available to consult was a list of 33 plant species prepared by the then Michigan Department of Conservation, called, "Living Beauty, Michigan's Rare Wildflowers." 27 of the plants grew in southern Michigan and all but two were found on the first five MNA preserves. (Only two remain on today's list of E-T-SC species.)

Tips from members and others were assiduously checked. Many resulted from asking two questions: "Do you know of any place with a lot of wildflowers?" and "Do you know of a place you would like to see preserved?"

It was not until 1973 that the Federal Endangered Species law was passed, followed the next year by the State law. At that time the criteria adopted for listing in Michigan became much more exacting and embraced plant species botanists seldom, if ever saw—for example, one found in less than five of the state's 83 counties.

In 1968, Robert Kilgore of Port Huron started botanizing for the MNA. Using several references, he arrived at 1795 native species known to occur within the state's borders (37 are now extinct). From this he compiled a "want list" of flora the MNA did not have on its preserves. The distinction between alien and native species was meticulously maintained.

Most unusual plants typically grow in undisturbed habitats. Although most common species were well represented in early MNA sanctuaries, rarer ones took considerable detective work to locate. MNA volunteers, however, were equal to the task, and the organization soon acquired several unique, ecologically important projects.

When I came on the scene in 1978, I found that Kilgore, while technically an amateur, had pursued a lifelong disciplined study of botany. He had thoroughly explored the majority of MNA's fifty-odd sanctuaries and maintained elaborate records. Upon Kilgore's retirement, I was privileged to receive and continue these records. Working with Bertha Daubendiek, Executive Director, I reviewed the MNA holdings, investigated the newer sanctuaries, and pursued new leads.

I found that the MNA labors had borne sweet fruit. They had resulted in the acquiring of top-notch wild lands—high quality examples of natural communities which also possessed beauty and a sense of wildness.

The goal of my work was to make an appraisal of the overall program and find what it lacked. It lacked very little! My detailed analysis was rewarded by some thrilling discoveries. The MNA's program protects samples of 29 of Michigan's 30 known natural habitats containing 82% of its native plant species. The preserves have 50% of the 342 species (snails, insects, amphibians, reptiles, and birds as well as plants) listed as "Endangered," "Threatened," or "of Special Concern." Virtually all of the state's native tree species are found on MNA lands, which also provide nesting habitat for 170 bird species. With regard to the remaining 18% of Michigan plant species, many have not been seen by botanists for years. Some species are known only from Isle Royale National Park or other publicly held lands. Dismissing these "unattainables," MNA's practical want list of plants is now reduced to around 100 species. Only 26 are in need of protection. Their acquisition continues to be one of MNA's objectives.

A tenet of confining field work to privately owned

The success of the program has depended on the work of dedicated volunteers. A deep-seated MNA policy has been that members cannot be paid. Here is Russ Hawken III, of Galesburg, gathering aquatic plants for sampling. "We're the younger generation the MNA looks to for carrying on its traditions."

properties has resulted in the ferreting out of many fine natural areas previously unknown to the scientific community and the process is still continuing. It takes hard work to find a site with the desired natural features, which is also acquirable. The MNA has continually faced a cold reality that for every 20 prospective sanctuary sites, perhaps only one has a willing seller or donor. The organization's success is truly the product of great perseverance.

One plant, the small whorled pogonia orchid, *Isotria medeoloides* (E, E-USA), is found in the state only on MNA land. MNA preserves have the second largest population in the USA of American hart's-tongue fern, *Phyllitis scolopendrium var. americana,* a candidate for federal listing. Five Lakes Muskegon Nature Sanctuary is the most celebrated coastal plains marsh in the state. Hill's thistle, *Cirsium hillii,* a regional endemic and candidate for federal listing, has been wiped out in other states in its original prairie habitat. Its presence on an MNA sand prairie is of national significance. In addition, the MNA has a project to preserve the habitat of the copperbellied water snake (E), a species currently under field review for federal listing.

A popular feature of the MNA program is that it provides more than one preserve where many typical Michigan wildflowers may be seen. A number of properties have the pink moccasin flower and trailing arbutus; two

have calypso orchids and dwarf lake iris; nine have ram's head orchids; and 25 have the exquisite fringed gentian—all the way from Lenawee County at the Ohio border up to Keweenaw in the Upper Peninsula. The same holds true for preserves available for the study of ferns (MNA has all but nine of the 104 Michigan fern species), native trees, and birds. I could go on and on. Of my own specialty, native violets, there are 24 Michigan varieties and MNA properties have all but one, which is found on a publicly owned island.

Since 1985, when this MNA "dreambook" was planned, Bertha and the photographers, after consulting my written descriptions, went out and earmarked where to take photos on MNA lands. The preserves abound in examples of Michigan's classic habitats, and because the easiest places to reach have been pin-pointed, any interested person can enjoy seeing and studying them himself.

Good hunting. I hope to meet you in the field.

Harvey E. Ballard, Jr.

87

Helmer Brook Prairie Plant Preserve (Mesic Black Soil)

1 *At the west edge of Battle Creek is this 10.07-acre jewel.* **The southern wet meadow** *ends at a dry knoll capped by a profusion of grasses and prairie wildflowers. Between the top of the knoll and its base is a mesic type of moist loam, fringed by prairie dock with its five foot tall daisy-like yellow flowers. The white flowers beneath the dock are flowering spurge; left of center are black-eyed Susans; center pink flowers are wild bergamot, and right of center are budded spikes of New England blazing star. Leiberg's panic grass (T), more than two feet tall (3), barely tops the huge basal leaves of the prairie dock. The fuzzy globular spikelets (2) are the flowers of this grass, at the stage when they are just exposing their yellow stamens.*

1

2

3

5

Southern Swamp Forest

4 *Swamp forests have standing water in them during most or all of the year. Tall sedges, ferns, and grasses often grow luxuriantly in the damp muck, and trees are buttressed with widely spreading raised roots, which allow the trees to "breathe" in the saturated soil. Walk along the east boundary of Columbia Nature Sanctuary in Jackson County on the paved Dearmyer Road, .2 mile north of County Line Road. Without getting your feet wet, if you peer in, you can immerse yourself visually in the depths of this high quality* **southern swamp forest.** *The tallest trees are swamp white oaks, with some red maples and small slippery elm trees.*

Dry Northern Forest

5 *Growing on sandy soils, the* **dry northern forest** *is largely composed of red and white pines, white spruce, and occasional hardwoods such as aspen and birch. Where the forest is dense, shrubs, herbs, and wildflowers are scarce, but where canopy trees have fallen, letting in sun, the open spaces fill in. Such a forest can easily be seen along the west end of Brockway Mountain Drive, north of Upson Lake Nature Sanctuary. At places you can look down into such a woods from your car. Red pine trunks are prominent as are the leaves of thimbleberry, right, and large-leaved aster, left. By looking on the map on page 93 you can place the area where this picture and the boreal forest picture page 72 were taken.*

6

6 *MNA preserves are prime places to learn about plant ecology. For instance, the distribution of the great-spurred violet, Viola selkirkii, is well represented on MNA land. This inconspicuous violet, distinct with its large spurs and shallowly toothed leaves, thrives in rich moist soil beneath conifers throughout the UP, but only grows north of the Bay City-Muskegon tension zone in the LP.*

An Historical Perspective

Michigan Nature Association is a nonprofit citizens' organization that began as a bird study group in 1951. It was incorporated in 1952 as the St. Clair Metropolitan Beach Sanctuary Association whose purpose was to persuade the Huron-Clinton Metropolitan Park Authority to change its plans to build a dance pavilion where thousands of common terns were attempting to nest. (Because the birds' usual breeding ground, Strawberry Island in Lake St. Clair, was under water due to abnormally high lake levels, the terns had chosen to nest on land created artificially by the park authority.) The area was posted as a state wildlife sanctuary, yet employees of the park, on orders, were mowing through the birds. The pressure of public opinion applied by the group, whose membership quickly grew to 500, soon brought a halt to the massacre.

In 1954, the organization became Macomb Nature Association, named for the county in which it was located. Macomb was then the fastest growing area in the greater Detroit region. Seeing nature "losing out" to development, the Association devoted the first six years of its existence to purely educational efforts. Being dissatisfied, however, with government and other conservation organizations' attitude of unconcern, it decided that the only way to save any nature in Michigan was to buy and own it outright. In 1959, the group sent a 15-page "white paper," outlining the need for decisive action, to 98 leading conservation groups in the state. Receiving no response, it decided to proceed independently and has continued to do so. Because Michigan law forbade anyone except the State to use the nomenclatures: "game refuge," "game preserve," "game reserve," or "wildlife sanctuary," the organization devised its own term, "nature sanctuary," a concept that has

1

2

been very well received. It contacted owners of 95 prospective nature properties and, finding five willing to sell, went into debt for the then unheard of sum of $15,000 in land contracts to establish its first preserves.

With two more name changes—in 1965, to Eastern Michigan Nature Association and in 1970, to Michigan Nature Association, the organization has now grown statewide in territory and influence. For the last 28 years it has been fund-raising continuously to preserve important natural areas in Michigan. It also sponsors field trips, programs, and publications to inform the public on conservation issues.

The Old and the New

1 *Since its first years, the Michigan Nature Association has annually prepared public information exhibits. This is one at the Michigan State Fair in 1985.*
2 *In 1970, three MNA member volunteers were among the most active in searching the state for new properties to preserve. They are pictured on an early exploratory trip to the western Upper Peninsula. At bottom center is Bertha Daubendiek, then a court reporter; standing behind her is Thelma Sonnenberg, a biology teacher; and Rita Juckett, a registered nurse.* Their guides in the Keweenaw were John Ollilia (in red) examining the exposed roots of a big yellow birch, and Dave Kennedy, both students from the biology department of what is now Michigan Tech at Houghton.*
*Bertha is still at the MNA helm; Thelma and Rita, after serving many years as officers and directors, now have Director Emeritus status as do outstanding MNA volunteers Bette Jane Wogen and Elizabeth Parsons.

Bloom Dates

"When does the blue-eyed Mary come out at Dowagiac Woods Nature Sanctuary? The dwarf lake iris at Beaver Tail Point Plant Preserve? The wild-lilac in the Keweenaw Peninsula?" Questions such as these are often directed to the MNA, which schedules many field trips for its members around expected blossoming times. How can a person find out when a favorite flower will be at its peak? Field guides are not much help, because they cover such a large section of the country and refer to a two to three month period. Instead, information and photographic dates given in this book for specific plants will prove much more accurate in planning your own wildflower hunts.

The floral season in Michigan starts in March with the odd-looking (and smelling) skunk cabbage, and ends in October when the witch-hazel displays its curly yellow petals. In between, there is a wide array—showing all colors of the rainbow. April begins in the woodlands with hepatica, bloodroot, harbinger-of-spring, and marsh marigold. Late April and May bring on a rush of wildflowers, trying to beat the trees as they leaf out. This stampede includes spring beauty, trout lily, Dutchman's breeches, red trillium, white trillium, blue-eyed Mary, wood poppy, violets, dwarf ginseng, Jack-in-the-pulpit, Virginia bluebells, Greek valerian, wild geranium, fringed polygala, star flower, and painted trillium. By mid-May some early prairie plants come into flower—hoary puccoon, lupine (3), and small white lady-slipper.

For many photographers, Memorial Day weekend is the time to make their annual trip to the Mackinac Bridge and beyond. At this time many orchids are out—calypso, ram's head, moccasin flower, and yellow lady-slipper—as well as other species such as dwarf lake iris, bird's eye primrose, and wild-lilac. Other orchids blooming in June are arethusa, showy lady-slipper, calopogon, and rose pogonia. By late June, Michigan and wood lilies are at their peak. July starts the color show of prairie flowers. By the

3

second half of August the lobelias—great blue and cardinal flower—come to perfection, along with jewelweed, closed and fringed gentians, and Michigan monkey-flower. From September on until frost, a crazy quilt of goldenrods and asters echo the gold and russet of the changing oaks and maples.

In spring, a bloom lag of six weeks may be expected, from the southern tier of counties to the Keweenaw. The reverse is true in fall; due to the shorter growing season up north, the flowers bloom earlier in their haste to set seed. Other factors can cause an expected bloom date to fluctuate. On any particular preserve, an identical species often blooms several days earlier if it is located in a protected spot with a southern exposure, than it will in an exposed north-facing situation, even though growing only a few yards away. The so-called "lake influence," meaning proximity to a large water mass such as one of the Great Lakes, may also result in earlier or later bloom dates than further inland.

Pages 31 and 32 of "The Nature Year in Macomb and St. Clair Counties, Michigan," published by the Association in 1963, is a good guide to average dates of bloom and other plant attractions in a large part of the state.

We hope you will be encouraged to keep your own records; reviewing them in winter and spring will furnish inspiration for many excursions in the field.

3 *Wild lupine,* Lupinus perennis, *is a common plant of the western states, and grows in dry, sandy, acid soil in the lower part of Michigan;(not found in the UP). It blooms mid-May at the MNA Sand Creek Prairie in Hillsdale county and at Five Lakes Muskegon.*

26 Easy-To-Visit Sanctuary Maps

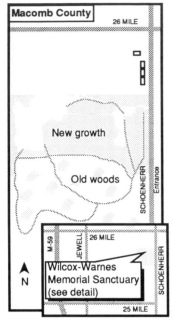

Macomb County

26 MILE

SCHOENHERR

New growth

Old woods

Entrance

SCHOENHERR

M-59 · JEWELL · 26 MILE

Wilcox-Warnes Memorial Sanctuary (see detail)

SCHOENHERR

25 MILE

N

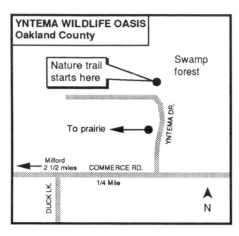

YNTEMA WILDLIFE OASIS
Oakland County

Nature trail starts here

Swamp forest

To prairie

YNTEMA DR.

Milford 2 1/2 miles

COMMERCE RD.

1/4 Mile

DUCK LK.

N

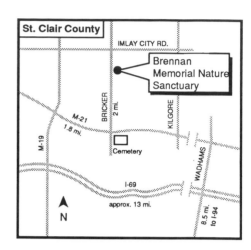

St. Clair County

IMLAY CITY RD.

Brennan Memorial Nature Sanctuary

BRICKER 2 mi.

KILGORE

WADHAMS

M-21 1.8 mi.

M-19

Cemetery

I-69

approx. 13 mi.

8.5 mi. to I-94

N

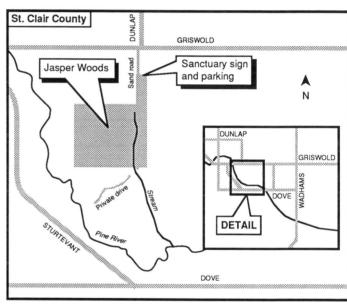

St. Clair County

DUNLAP

GRISWOLD

Jasper Woods

Sand road

Sanctuary sign and parking

N

DUNLAP

GRISWOLD

DOVE

WADHAMS

Private drive

Stream

DETAIL

STURTEVANT

Pine River

DOVE

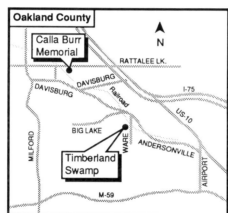

Oakland County

N

Calla Burr Memorial

RATTALEE LK.

DAVISBURG

DAVISBURG

Railroad

I-75

US-10

MILFORD

BIG LAKE

WARE

ANDERSONVILLE

AIRPORT

Timberland Swamp

M-59

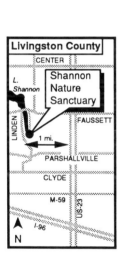

Livingston County

CENTER

L. Shannon

Shannon Nature Sanctuary

LINDEN

1 mi.

FAUSSETT

PARSHALLVILLE

CLYDE

M-59

US-23

I-96

N

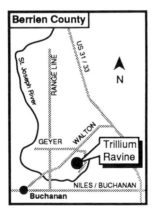

Berrien County

US 31 / 33

St. Joseph River

RANGE LINE

GEYER

WALTON

Trillium Ravine

NILES / BUCHANAN

Buchanan

N

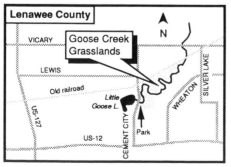

Lenawee County

VICARY

Goose Creek Grasslands

LEWIS

Old railroad

US-127

CEMENT CITY

Little Goose L.

Park

US-12

WHEATON

SILVER LAKE

N

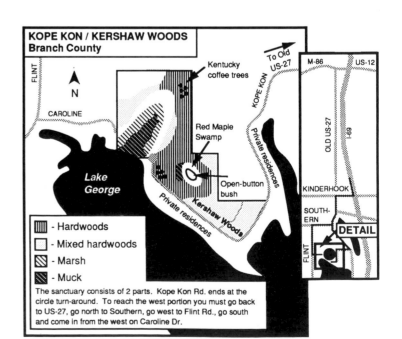

KOPE KON / KERSHAW WOODS
Branch County

FLINT

CAROLINE

N

To Old US-27

Kentucky coffee trees

M-86

US-12

Lake George

Red Maple Swamp

Open-button bush

KOPE KON

Private residences

OLD US-27

I-69

Private residences

Kershaw Woods

KINDERHOOK

SOUTHERN

FLINT

DETAIL

▨ - Hardwoods
□ - Mixed hardwoods
▧ - Marsh
▩ - Muck

The sanctuary consists of 2 parts. Kope Kon Rd. ends at the circle turn-around. To reach the west portion you must go back to US-27, go north to Southern, go west to Flint Rd., go south and come in from the west on Caroline Dr.

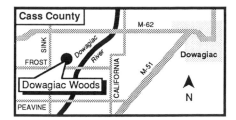

Cass County

SINK
FROST
Dowagiac River
M-62
Dowagiac
California
M-51
PEAVINE
Dowagiac Woods
N

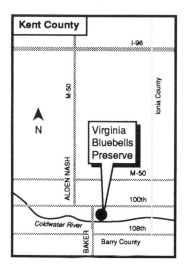

Kent County

I-96
M-50
Ionia County
Alden Nash
Baker
N
Virginia Bluebells Preserve
M-50
100th
Coldwater River
108th
Barry County

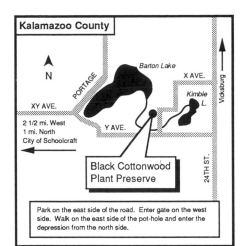

Kalamazoo County

N
Barton Lake
X AVE.
Kimble L.
XY AVE.
PORTAGE
Y AVE.
Vicksburg
24TH ST.
2 1/2 mi. West
1 mi. North
City of Schoolcraft
Black Cottonwood Plant Preserve

Park on the east side of the road. Enter gate on the west side. Walk on the east side of the pot-hole and enter the depression from the north side.

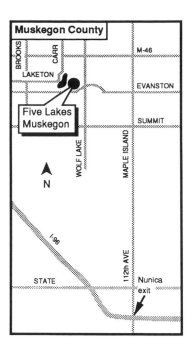

Muskegon County

BROOKS
CARR
M-46
LAKETON
EVANSTON
Five Lakes Muskegon
SUMMIT
WOLF LAKE
MAPLE ISLAND
N
I-96
112th AVE
Nunica exit
STATE

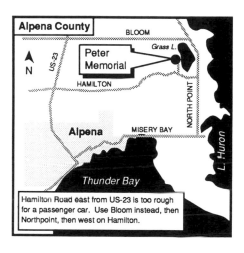

Alpena County

BLOOM
US-23
Peter Memorial
Grass L.
HAMILTON
NORTH POINT
Alpena
MISERY BAY
L. Huron
N
Thunder Bay

Hamilton Road east from US-23 is too rough for a passenger car. Use Bloom instead, then Northpoint, then west on Hamilton.

Antrim County

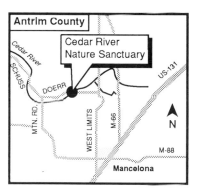

Cedar River Nature Sanctuary
Cedar River
SCHUSS
DOERR
MTN. RD.
WEST LIMITS
US-131
M-66
N
M-88
Mancelona

St. Joseph County

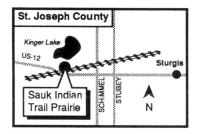

Kinger Lake
US-12
Sturgis
SCHIMMEL
STUBEY
N
Sauk Indian Trail Prairie

Newaygo County

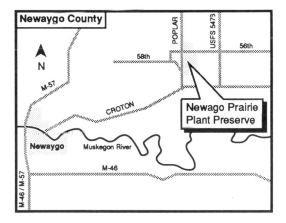

N
POPLAR
USFS 5473
56th
58th
M-57
CROTON
Newago Prairie Plant Preserve
Newaygo
Muskegon River
M-46
M-46 / M-57

Alger County

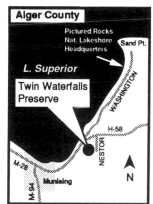

Pictured Rocks Nat. Lakeshore Headquarters
Sand Pt.
L. Superior
WASHINGTON
Twin Waterfalls Preserve
H-58
M-28
NESTOR
N
M-94
Munising

Mackinac County

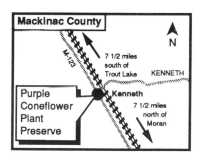

M-123
7 1/2 miles south of Trout Lake
KENNETH
N
Purple Coneflower Plant Preserve
Kenneth
7 1/2 miles north of Moran

Mackinac County

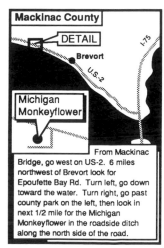

DETAIL
Brevort
I-75
US-2
Michigan Monkeyflower

From Mackinac Bridge, go west on US-2. 6 miles northwest of Brevort look for Epoufette Bay Rd. Turn left, go down toward the water. Turn right, go past county park on the left, then look in next 1/2 mile for the Michigan Monkeyflower in the roadside ditch along the north side of the road.

Keweenaw Peninsula

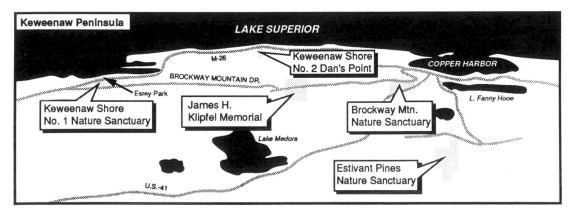

LAKE SUPERIOR
M-26
Keweenaw Shore No. 2 Dan's Point
COPPER HARBOR
BROCKWAY MOUNTAIN DR.
Esrey Park
L. Fanny Hooe
Keweenaw Shore No. 1 Nature Sanctuary
James H. Klipfel Memorial
Brockway Mtn. Nature Sanctuary
Lake Medora
Estivant Pines Nature Sanctuary
U.S.-41

93

- Easy to visit sanctuaries

- Niagaran Formation

N

Sanctuary Index

For further information consult the 1983 MNA Sanctuary Guidebook, updated, or call the MNA Business Office: 1-313-324-2626.

Persons mentioned

Past Presidents of MNA

Louis Senghas
Cass Kierblewski
Thelma Sonnenberg
Bette Jane Wogen
James Norton
Richard W. Holzman
Larry Kastler
Edna S. Newnan
Ruth North
Judy Kelly
Robert Pleznac

1952 St. Clair Metropolitan Beach Sanctuary Association.
1955 Macomb Nature Association.
1965 Eastern Michigan Nature Association.
1970 Michigan Nature Association.

Additional Information

Reference Sources

The Vegetation of Wisconsin, An Ordination of Plant Communities, John T. Curtis, 1959. The University of Wisconsin Press, Box 1379, Madison, Wisconsin 53701.

The Michigan Botanist, Vol. 19, No. 3, May, 1980, "Nature Preserves in Michigan, 1920-1979," Susan R. Crispin, Michigan Natural Features Inventory.

"Michigan's Special Plants—Endangered, Threatened, Special Concern, and Probably Extirpated, January, 1988," list produced by the Endangered Species Program of the Michigan Department of Natural Resources and the Michigan Natural Features Inventory.

"Michigan's Special Animals—Endangered, Threatened, Special Concern, and Probably Extirpated, January, 1988," list produced by the Nongame and Endangered Species Programs of the Michigan Department of Natural Resources and the Michigan Natural Features Inventory.

Michigan Nature Association Publications

The Nature Year in Macomb and St. Clair Counties, Michigan, 1963. A 64-page booklet including nature lore, lists of flora and fauna, and illustrated with black and white ink drawings, maps, and photographs.

Michigan Nature Association Sanctuary Guidebook, 1983, updated. The most complete source of detailed preserve information, the Guidebook features 126 pages with 65,000 words of text on natural history information written by laymen for laymen. It covers Michigan's native wildlife, contains over 450 beautiful black and white photographs of plants, mammals, birds, and habitats, and includes complete instructions and maps for visiting the sanctuaries.

Michigan Nature Association

is a nonprofit organization whose purpose is to carry on a program of natural history study and conservation education and to acquire, maintain, and protect nature sanctuaries, natural areas, and plant preserves in the State of Michigan or areas adjacent thereto. Anyone interested in the aims and activities of the organization may join. You do not have to be a member to contribute.

For membership information and to order publications, contact:

Michigan Nature Association Business Office
7981 Beard Road, Box 102
Avoca, MI 48006
(313) 324-2626

MNA welcomes gifts of money, land or other property, or securities, to use in its program. For consultation regarding such gifts, which are federally income tax deductible, please contact: Bertha Daubendiek, (313) 324-2626; or James R. Buschmann, Counsel for MNA, (313) 393-7507.

(Above) male Canada goose defending family. (Opposite) View of Pine River with autumn maple leaves, Brennan Memorial Nature Sanctuary.

Habitats Pictured

Forests (8 of 12)
CONIFER SWAMP

Rich conifer swamp
p.48 Lost Lake N.S.
pp.88, 89 Columbia N.S.

Poor conifer swamp
p.55 Grass Lake N.S.

SOUTHERN SWAMP FOREST
SOUTHERN FLOODPLAIN FOREST
p.26 Powell Mem. N.S.

MESIC NORTHERN FOREST
(yellow birch-hemlock-maple)
p.19 Jasper Woods N.S.

MESIC SOUTHERN FOREST
(beech-maple)
p.20 Brennan Mem. N.S., p.29
p.40 Trillium Ravine P.P.

DRY MESIC SOUTHERN FOREST
(oak-hickory)
p.29
p.28 Adeline Kershaw Woods N.S.

DRY NORTHERN FOREST
pp.76, 89 Upson Lake N.S.

NORTHERN BOREAL FOREST
p.76 Keweenaw Shore No. 1 N.S.

Wetlands (4 of 6)
MARSH
p.29 Mentioned

COASTAL PLAIN MARSH
p.42 Five Lakes Muskegon N.S.
pp.46, 47 Barvicks Sand Dunes N.S.

OPEN BOG
p.41 Pennfield Bog N.S.
Muskeg
p.67 Soo Muskeg N.S.

WET MEADOW p.29
Northern wet meadow
pp.48, 49 Lost Lake N.S.

Southern wet meadow
pp.12, 13 Lakeville Swamp N.S.
p.24 Goose Creek Grasslands N.S.
p.88 Helmer Brook Prairie P.P.

Sand habitats (2)
SAND/GRAVEL BEACH
p.57 Lake Superior N.S.

OPEN/SAND DUNES
pp.46, 47 Barvicks Sand Dunes N.S.
p.59 Lake Superior N.S.
pp.62, 63 Lake Huron Sand Dunes P.P.

Rock habitats (3 of 4)
BEDROCK BEACH p.29
p.72 Keweenaw Shore No. 1 N.S.
p.79 Keweenaw Shore No. 2 P.P. (Dan's Point)
also nearby Hylton Mem. P.P.

Cobble beach
pp.64, 65 Harvey's Rocks (Drummond Island)

ROCK FORMATIONS
Bald
p.81 Klipfel Mem. N.S.
p.84 Grinnell Mem. N.S.
Rock escarpment
pp.70, 71 Justeson Mem. N.S.
Boulder field
p.61 Rare Fern P.P.
Sandstone conglomerate
p.81 Klipfel Mem. N.S.
pp.68, 69 Daubendiek Mem. P.P.

ALVAR (open alvar)

Prairies (3 of 5)
MESIC BLACK SOIL PRAIRIE
p.37 Sauk Indian Trail Prairie P.P.
p.88 Helmer Brook Prairie P.P.

DRY SAND PRAIRIE
pp.34, 35 Newaygo Prairie N.S.

MESIC SAND PRAIRIE
p.91 Sand Creek Prairie P.P.

NOT PICTURED

Forests
HARDWOOD-CONIFER SWAMP
No. 85 Barvicks Sand Dunes N.S.
No. 59 Wade Mem. N.S.

DRY-MESIC NORTHERN FOREST
No. 47 Jasper Woods on higher, drier land
above the mesic northern forest

DRY SOUTHERN FOREST
No. 73 Wulfenia (Fitch) P.P., mostly black
and white oaks

PINE BARREN
No. 64 Soo Muskeg N.S.
No. 78 Daubendiek Mem. P.P.

Wetlands
MARSH
No. 25 Lefglen N.S. and
No. 67 Roach Point N.S.

INTERDUNAL WETLAND
No. 61 Frink's Pond P.P.
WOODED DUNE AND
SWALE COMPLEX
No. 28 Lake Huron Sand Dunes P.P.

Rock
BEDROCK GLADE
No. 31 Zeerip Mem. P.P. (Drummond Island)

Prairies
HILLSIDE PRAIRIE
No. 73 Wulfenia (Fitch) P.P.
OAK OPENING/WOODLAND PRAIRIE
No. 39 Chen Mem. Prairie P.P.

19 habitats shown plus 10 above=29. A 30th habitat of Michigan, INLAND SALT MARSH, is not on any MNA property. The only good example is in the State-owned Maple River Game Area.